Morning Classroom Conversations

We dedicate this book to all of the educators who see the future of our society in the children we educate today.

Morning Classroom Conversations

Build Your Students' Social-Emotional, Character, and Communication Skills Every Day

Maurice J. Elias

Nina A. Murphy

Kellie A. McClain

Foreword by Joshua Freedman

A SAGE Publishing Company

FOR INFORMATION:

Corwin
A SAGE Company
2455 Teller Road
Thousand Oaks, California 91320
(800) 233-9936
www.corwin.com

SAGE Publications Ltd.
1 Oliver's Yard
55 City Road
London EC1Y 1SP
United Kingdom

SAGE Publications India Pvt. Ltd.
B 1/I 1 Mohan Cooperative Industrial Area
Mathura Road, New Delhi 110 044
India

SAGE Publications Asia-Pacific Pte. Ltd.
18 Cross Street #10-10/11/12
China Square Central
Singapore 048423

President: Mike Soules
Associate Vice President and
    Editorial Director: Monica Eckman
Publisher: Jessica Allan
Senior Content Development
    Editor: Lucas Schleicher
Associate Content Development
    Editor: Mia Rodriguez
Production Editor: Melanie Birdsall
Copy Editor: Exeter Premedia Services
Typesetter: Exeter Premedia Services
Proofreader: Wendy Jo Dymond
Indexer: Exeter Premedia Services
Cover Designer: Scott Van Atta
Marketing Manager: Olivia Bartlett

Printed in the United States of America

Library of Congress Control Number: 2021938742

ISBN 978-1-0718-3936-2

This book is printed on acid-free paper.

21 22 23 24 25 10 9 8 7 6 5 4 3 2 1

Contents

8 THREE-YEAR DEVELOPMENTAL PROGRESSION   114

9 IMPLEMENTATION CONSIDERATIONS FOR LEAD TEACHERS AND/OR ADMINISTRATORS   124

 Visit the companion website at
resources.corwin.com/MorningClassroomConversations
for downloadable resources.

Foreword

Decades later, I can still feel the thrill of my favorite class in high school. Our teacher, Mr. Barankin, would unleash one of life's big questions, give an impish grin as he saw us begin to grapple, and tip his chair back against the chalkboard to listen. These deep questions became guides throughout my life, encouraging me to think more deeply about meaning, purpose, beauty, and my role in the world.

Those conversations are one reason why, when I later became a teacher, I treasured classes where my students and I would engage in discussions about deep topics, sharing views about everything from the meaning of courage to which character on the sitcom-of-the-season we liked the most. At the time, I felt the significance of this kind of conversation, but I didn't know why, or the essential social-emotional skills that we exercised together.

Just as the questions in Barry Barankin's class have resonated with me, I've been honored to hear similar feelings from my students. The kids I taught as adolescents are now "grown-ups"; many of them have become parents, and I still hear from some of them. They don't remember the brilliant lectures I delivered, but they do remember when our class sat under a tree and talked about values, what they cared about, and what they hoped to do in the world.

Fast-forward: Today, a growing body of research shows that those social-emotional skills are not only useful for personal development, they're actually central to academic learning too.[1] Alarmingly, these skills are also declining globally.[2] In addition to research, we can see the effects in headlines about increased social and political polarization in country after country around the globe: We are more volatile and less willing or able to listen to one another.

---

[1] Where we once saw social-emotional skills as useful for intrapersonal and interpersonal growth, the neuroscience of learning reveals they're actually foundational for academic learning as well. For more on this, see my interview with cognitive neuroscientist Mary Helen Immordino Yang (https://www.6seconds.org/2020/09/15/neuroscience-learning/).

[2] In the world's largest study of emotional intelligence, using a randomized sample from over 126 countries, skills such as emotional awareness, emotion management, and empathy have declined significantly over the last decade. See https://6sec.org/soh for the current data.

The rise of social media is likely one reason for this decline. There's evidence to hypothesize that increased use of digital platforms is part of the erosion of civility. Teens who use social media more are actually more lonely—less socially engaged.[3] An "extractive attention economy" has developed, based on taking our attention: According to the Center for Humane Technology, big-tech algorithms are designed to create dissatisfaction and provide volatility to increase the use of social media platforms while reducing individual well-being as well as civil behavior.[4] Whatever the cause, we're facing a tidal wave of anxiety and loneliness, especially among young people.[5]

Meanwhile, as scores on empathy and collaboration decline globally, more and more businesses are calling these the essential skills of the future. Google's Chief Innovation Evangelist Frederik G. Pferdt said, "Empathy is the skill of the future."[6] The World Economic Forum's Future of Jobs reports in 2018 and 2020 highlighted that in an era of rapid transformation, the future of work will require both cognitive/technical skills and social-emotional skills.

For a decade, I've led a research project to track awareness about emotions as part of workplace performance. Surveys from over 95 countries have shown, over and over, that the biggest challenges managers face are relational.[7] While technical and business skills are important, what holds leaders back is a deficit in the social-emotional domain. These are the kinds of skills we develop through meaningful conversation.

In short, we have a massive and growing need for social-emotional skills.

Imagine a world where students are meaningfully engaged in practicing those skills. I run one of the world's largest nonprofit organizations working in this space. It's called Six Seconds, and our vision is a billion people practicing the skills of emotional intelligence. We measure and teach

---

[3] Jean Twenge has done extensive research on this link, such as Jean M. Twenge, W. Keith Campbell, Associations between screen time and lower psychological well-being among children and adolescents: Evidence from a population-based study, *Preventive Medicine Reports*, 12 (2018): 271–283, https://doi.org/10.1016/j.pmedr.2018.10.003.

[4] See the EmotionAI conference (www.6seconds.org/emotionai) and the Center for Humane Technology (humanetech.com).

[5] For a snapshot of trends on emotional well-being in the world, see www.6seconds.org/emotional-intelligence/topics/wellbeing/.

[6] See accelerate.withgoogle.com/stories/product-inclusion-leadership-insights-from-google-chief-innovation-evangelist-frederik-g-pferdt.

[7] See the Workplace Vitality research reports on 6sec.org/vitality.

a process for doing so—at work, at school, at home, and in communities. There are three steps to this process:

1. Being more aware
2. Making more careful and conscious choices
3. Stepping forward with both empathy and commitment to purpose.

There are many conversation topics in *Morning Classroom Conversations* that align to these steps. As educators and students engage in meaningful conversations about emotions, behaviors, and options, we'll have an opportunity to increase awareness. By "talking it out," we'll have a chance to expand options. Through dialogue around aspirations and values, we might be able to connect to that larger sense of purpose that could motivate us all to be better versions of ourselves.

While there are many programs that can teach social-emotional skills, I'd contend that the heart of this book isn't about explicit curriculum. Most curriculum is static; it's mass-produced and simplistic. It's usually instructor-driven and cognitive. Even well-intentioned social-emotional learning curricula can be boring—and, too often, white-centered and reinforcing transactional behavior norms.[8]

This brings us to the beauty of *Morning Classroom Conversations*. There are three features of this framework I'd like to highlight:

1. This is an approachable approach. Educators who read this book will quickly see that these conversations draw on "the usual" pedagogical skills we use every day, such as inquiry, analysis, and communication.
2. It's student-centered. The questions in *Morning Classroom Conversations* are ones where students are the experts. Rather than asking about what's in a text or what the teacher thinks, this book is full of questions about students' perceptions and experiences.
3. These are big, meaningful questions. All too often, classroom conversations are about important-but-not-profound topics. Dates. Formulae. Items that can be easily assessed on a multiple-choice test. While these may have utility, they're limited. Big questions, however, can engage levels of curiosity, discovery, and meaning that go far deeper.

---

[8] The Communities for Just Schools Fund published a powerful article on this topic: "When SEL Is Used As Another Form of Policing" (medium.com/@justschools/when-sel-is-used-as-another-form-of-policing-fa53cf85dce4). Cierra Kahler-Jones, one of the authors, added additional perspectives in this video: www.youtube.com/watch?v=N_d_YSH9DhA.

1. AN APPROACHABLE APPROACH

You can do this! The frameworks in this book are not introducing some new or foreign language. The practices that the authors are advocating here will feel natural and practical for most educators. What's remarkable and new is a simple way to take our typical educational practices to a deeper level.

The book offers ways to adapt the process to a variety of contexts. I suspect many educators will enjoy just randomly flipping to a page to get an inspiring question to discuss today!

The point is that this isn't a typical "packaged program." It's a framework that is adaptable and will support both your academic and social-emotional learning.

2. STUDENT-CENTERED

The obvious way to escape from culturally insensitive curricula that reinforce systems of oppression (racism, sexism, classism, etc.) is to put your students and their lived experience at the center of learning. What we call upon as "factual evidence" is usually rooted in specific cultural understandings. In this book, you'll find questions that open up equity-oriented dialogue where the students' expertise is meaningful, such as

- Where do you feel like your voice is heard? Are there places where you wish your voice was heard more?
- Why might people not listen to new ideas? What helps you to be more likely to listen to new or different ideas?
- A new student just arrived at your school. What do you think it feels like to be living in a new place with all new people?

These are questions that kids can answer from their own cultural perspective, norms, and values, and in discussing these, adults and youth will increase their mutual understanding.

3. BIG, MEANINGFUL QUESTIONS

As an author of an assessment of school climate,[9] I'm concerned about how students and educators feel about school. We summarize this into an index of engagement; we'd know students are engaged if they look forward to going to school. In a global study of over 2,000 adolescents, we found *no* students were meaningfully engaged.[10]

One solution is to make time to pose questions that students will want to discuss. The previous examples are questions that, as an educator, I'd love to discuss. I'm genuinely curious about what students would say. How about you?

I started with the story of my favorite high school teacher asking big questions. I can imagine a generation from now, people will look back at their *Morning Classroom Conversations* and reminisce about how these meaningful questions became guides in their lives. This book is chock-a-block-full of the kinds of questions that will lead you to those life-changing interactions.

—**Joshua Freedman**, MCC, CEO of The Six Seconds
Emotional Intelligence Network

---

[9] Education Vital Signs is a normed, validated measure of school climate, including dimensions such as safety and inclusion (see 6sec.org/evs).
[10] https://www.6seconds.org/2016/04/14/groundbreaking-education-research-area/.

Acknowledgments

We recognize that our work stands on the foundation of many others in the fields of school psychology, social-emotional learning, community psychology, and prevention. We have had colleagues, mentors, students, and collaborators too numerous to mention, whom we hold in great admiration and gratitude. The work in this book emerged from a specific project, Mastering Our Skills and Inspiring Character (MOSAIC), and there are some individuals whose work has found its way into the ideas and interventions we provide. Specifically, we want to thank our MOSAIC team, Arielle Linsky, Danielle Hatchimonji, Samantha Kifer, Sarah DeMarchena, Samual Nayman, Anam Ahsan, and Karen Colello and our many school colleagues, especially Franklin Walker, Paula Christen, Rosalyn Barnes, Robert Brower, Margaret Critelli, Francine Luce, and Joanna Veloz and all school staff who took on leadership roles within this program.

We also want to recognize the support of the Rutgers Social-Emotional and Character Development Lab and the many individuals therein, largely talented undergraduates, who worked with data, organized intervention materials, and kept the website working optimally.

Of course, we owe a debt of gratitude to family, other loved ones, and friends, who gave us time and space to do the work this book describes, who inspired us, and believed in us. They have been the wind beneath our wings. And we would be remiss without also extending thanks to Jessica Allan, Mia Rodriguez, and Lucas Schleicher, from Corwin, who shared our enthusiasm and lent their editorial and literary expertise to help our ideas become clearer, more organized, and accessible, and visually presentable. We could not have asked for a better publishing team.

Finally, we thank all of our readers, past, present, and future. Your practical suggestions constantly improve the effectiveness of Morning Classroom Conversations (MCC), and we encourage you to send your suggestions and improvements to us at MorningClassroomConversations@gmail.com. We will be posting new ideas, resources, and answers to some of the readers' questions at this book's website, resources.corwin.com/MorningClassroomConversations, periodically so you can bring the best of them to your students in a constantly refreshed way. We are excited to be alongside you on your MCC journey!

PUBLISHER'S ACKNOWLEDGMENTS

Corwin gratefully acknowledges the contributions of the following reviewers:

Jessica Baldwin
High School Teacher
Claxton High School
Claxton, GA

Elizabeth Crane
Adjunct Professor
University of Cumberlands
Lexington, KY

Darilyn Gorton
ELA Teacher
Warwick Public Schools
Warwick, RI

Johanna Josaphat
Educator/Teacher Leader
The Urban Assembly Unison School
Brooklyn, NY

Marianne L. Lescher
School Principal
Kyrene Traditional Academy
Chandler, AZ

Louis Lim
Vice-Principal
Richmond Green Secondary School
Richmond Hill, Ontario, Canada

Laura Schaffer Metcalfe
Education Faculty
Grand Canyon University
Phoenix, AZ

Patricia Long Tucker
Regional Superintendent-Retired
District of Columbia Public Schools
Washington, DC

About the Authors

Maurice J. Elias, PhD, is Professor, Psychology Department, Rutgers University, Director, Social-Emotional and Character Development Lab (www .secdlab.org), Co-Director of the Rutgers-based Academy for SEL in Schools, which offers online certificates in SEL Instruction and School Leadership (SELinSchools.org), and a member of the Leadership Team for SEL4NJ and SEL4US (www.SEL4US .org). He received the Joseph E. Zins Memorial Senior Scholar Award for Social-Emotional Learning from CASEL, the Sanford McDonnell Award for Lifetime Achievement in Character Education, and the Jane Bostrum Service to School Psychology Award. Dr. Elias is a past winner of the Lela Rowland Prevention Award, the Ernest McMahon Class of 1930 Award for service to New Jersey, and the American Psychological Association/Society for Community Research and Action's Distinguished Contribution to Practice and Ethnic Minority Mentoring awards. His books include *Emotionally Intelligent Parenting, The Educator's Guide to Emotional Intelligence and Academic Achievement: Social-Emotional Learning in the Classroom,* and *The Other Side of the Report Card: Assessing Students' Social, Emotional, and Character Development* (how schools and districts can integrate social-emotional and character development systematically into their ongoing student report cards). Most recently, he is the coauthor of *The Joys & Oys of Parenting: Insights and Wisdom From the Jewish Tradition, Boost Emotional Intelligence in Students: 30 Flexible Research-Based Lessons to Build EQ Skills, Nurturing Students' Character: Everyday Teaching Activities for Social-Emotional Learning,* and *Social-Emotional Learning Lab: A Comprehensive SEL Resource Kit* (with Victoria Poedubicky).

He writes a blog on SECD for Edutopia (www.edutopia.org/profile/maurice-j-elias) and can be reached at secdlab@gmail.com. His Twitter handles are @SELinSchools and @SECDLab.

Take a look at a review on *The Other Side of the Report Card* from the New Jersey Association of School Psychologists at https://us.corwin.com/sites/default/files/review_of_the_other_side_njasp_0.pdf.

 **Nina A. Murphy, PsyD,** is a practicing school psychologist in Three Village Central School District, adjunct professor at St. Joseph's College, and Senior Consulting and Field Expert at the Social-Emotional and Character Development (SECD) Lab at Rutgers University. Dr. Murphy has had a commitment to supporting positive youth development since she can remember but learned, during her graduate work at Rutgers Graduate School of Applied and Professional Psychology and in the SECD Lab that this passion was targeted in helping youth develop positive character and purpose. She worked as a consultant in an urban school, opening her eyes to the intricacies of systems-level work and the importance of collaborative change.

Dr. Murphy has worked as a school psychologist for Grades K through 12 and feels inspired each day by the potential of her students to be the leaders of the future. Whether facilitating groups, individually counseling, consulting with teachers, coaching parents, or engaging in committee discussions, Dr. Murphy embeds her passion for social-emotional learning and development within each part of her work. At St. Joseph's College, she teaches classes based on adolescent development and personality, which align with her passion for supporting student growth.

Dr. Murphy's research targets youth leadership, self-efficacy, perseverance of effort, and student voice. She has trained teachers, administrators, and fellow psychologists in social-emotional curricula, embedding behavioral, emotional, and social competence into multitiered systems of supports and formulating social-emotional character development plans. Dr. Murphy has presented at conferences such as the National Association for School Psychology and APA Division 36 (Religion and Spirituality). She has been published in professional journals such as *The Middle School Journal* and *Evaluation and Program Planning,* highlighting a preventive youth leadership "Ambassador" program and the importance of preparing youth for social action. With experience in training youth leaders and supporting the implementation of social-emotional curricula, she is committed to ensuring youth establish positive character skills through programming and intentional, coordinated school supports.

Kellie A. McClain, PsyD, is a practicing school psychologist for the River Edge School District and a Senior Consulting and Field Expert at the Social-Emotional and Character Development (SECD) Lab at Rutgers University. She earned her doctoral and master's degrees in School Psychology from Fairleigh Dickinson University and a Bachelor's degree with a dual major in Psychology and Criminal Justice from Rutgers University. It was through these years of study that Dr. McClain developed a passion for helping at-risk youth through preventive measures. This passion is what led her to become a curriculum writer and consultant for the MOSAIC program, a social-emotional learning (SEL) program that helped bring Morning Classroom Conversations to life. Over a three-year span, Dr. McClain worked closely with students and teachers in multiple MOSAIC pilot schools and consulted around what is now known as *Morning Classroom Conversations*.

Dr. McClain's experience working with students and teachers in urban areas has further deepened her passion to provide children with the tools they need to succeed both within and beyond the classroom. Dr. McClain actively incorporates several SEL and SECD strategies in her current daily work as a school psychologist, with children ages 5 to 21. She specializes in professional development training with middle school teachers and administrators who are looking to incorporate SEL into their students' learning in a cohesive, systematic way.

Dr. McClain's research on the effects that student–teacher relationships have on SEL and academic achievement was published recently in the journal *Research in Middle Level Education*. Dr. McClain is committed to using her knowledge and experience to continue to help educators prepare students to tap into their full potential and live successful and purposeful lives.

CHAPTER 1

The Art of Conversation

Building and Reinforcing SEL Skills and Civil Discourse

> *Deeper conversations help people become explicable to each other and themselves. You can't really know yourself until you know how you express yourself and find yourself in another's eyes. Deeper conversation builds trust, the oxygen of society, exactly what we're missing right now.*

David Brooks, *New York Times*, **November 20, 2020, p. A27**

When was the last time you had a powerful conversation that felt like the "oxygen" referred to above? Who was it with and what made the conversation have depth? How did you feel after the conversation ended?

The art of conversation—which is increasingly becoming a lost art—is something that dates back thousands of years and continues to be necessary for a positive outcome across most areas of life. Anyone trying to make a friend, get a job, find a partner, or even play certain video games will find their chances of success and enjoyment improved by effective conversational skills. These are skills that must be explicitly taught, reinforced, and supported throughout development. Students need these skills now and in the future.

The implications of conversations held within organizations have been examined by many researchers, including Perkins

(2003). They found that the kinds of conversations held can move organizations forward or backward. Forward-moving conversations, such as "foster cohesiveness of the group, leaving people feeling good about working together and looking forward to doing more together" (2003, p. 20), are especially important in times of stress, which unfortunately characterize so many classrooms and schools now. Perkins also distinguishes between conversations that are structured, directed, purposeful, respectful, and challenging and those that are superficial, disconnected, unfocused, and talk for the sake of talk; he refers to the latter as "coblabulation" (2003, p. 149).

Sadly, many advisory period and homeroom chat times come closer to coblabulation than purposeful conversation. Fullan (2005) points out that while general conversation times can be useful and feel positive, they don't strongly contribute to building a positive classroom culture. Following Fullan's analysis, this book was written to help improve upon the "oxygen" of classroom culture by promoting students' social, emotional, and character development. As you'll learn, this can happen in as little as 10 to 15 minutes daily by engaging students in systematic, strategic, thought-and-emotion provoking conversations in the classroom—what we call Morning Classroom Conversations (MCCs).

When conducted consistently over the course of a year, MCCs get students thinking about the world around them and their own opinions and values and create curiosity about what their classmates are thinking, feeling, and aspiring to do. When experienced over three years, MCCs have the potential to transform how students view themselves, their classmates, and learning. When conducted across multiple classrooms and grade levels, the conversations can be catalysts for transforming a school's climate and culture.

 REVISITING CONVERSATIONS YOU HAVE HAD

The word "conversation" is defined in most dictionaries as "a talk, especially an informal one, between two or more people, in which news and ideas are exchanged." The key elements here are "exchanged" and "news"—implying shared familiarity and, derivationally, making what is familiar to one person, familiar to the other also. However, the *value* of conversation goes far beyond the exchange of information. What makes conversations so important in human interaction?

Stop and think for a moment …

Reflect on conversations you have had. What made your best conversations "genuine"? Did you feel heard/understood? Why? Did you want to talk to that person (or group of people) again soon? What about conversations that were non-genuine or unsatisfying? What was different about them? Let's take a closer look.

It is likely in this reflection, you thought of terms like "empathy," "emotional," "compassion," "gratitude," or similar words. An effective conversation includes reciprocal discussion that allows for all individuals involved to feel heard and understood. When reflecting on a conversation, you might consider the following questions to determine if the conversation was genuine:

1. *Social etiquette:* Did the participants create a safe space, both figuratively and physically, for communicating? For instance, was personal space given? Was each person able to speak without being interrupted?

2. *Clarity:* Did participants express thoughts in a clear manner? Were inquiries made by the listener(s) to further expand understanding?

3. *Reciprocation:* Were both individuals allowed to share their "truth" and demonstrate vulnerability? Were all opinions recognized, respected, and validated?

4. *Interest and engagement:* How did you know that the other person was interested/uninterested in what you had to say? Consider verbal communication and nonverbal cues.

5. *Perspective taking:* Did all participants consider how others might feel? If power or status differentials were present, how were they acknowledged, monitored, and potentially adjusted?

6. *Common ground*: Were commonalities found, even among differences?

These six core sets of questions, though not an exhaustive list, can be helpful in a reflective way when revisiting old conversations. On the other hand, if you are planning to become a better communicator in the future, could these questions also be used in a preparatory sense? Of course! In fact, if you are to review these questions before entering a conversation, it is much more likely that you will be aware of your behavior and respond in a more genuine way. Additionally, these questions are a great self-monitoring tool during conversations. For instance, let's say you are in a faculty meeting where you were asked to break out into groups. You notice that your group is being particularly negative and you feel like you disagree with everything being said. By reviewing the aforementioned questions, you can think about ways to include all voices, model vulnerability by sharing your feelings, and do your best to find commonalities, even among differences. Ideally, your group members will notice the effort you are putting into fostering genuine conversation and will be more likely to respond positively and reciprocate your actions.

Using these tools helps in facilitating communication for adults, and the same is true for your students. In Appendix D, we provide rubrics that allow Conversation Leaders and students to track progress with regard to learning the components of good conversations, developing social-emotional learning (SEL) skills, and achieving positive outcomes as a result of engaging in MCCs. As with all things (think about how you learned how to drive!), what you focus on becomes a habit that runs like a program in the background. The same applies to students, of course. Guiding youth in effective conversations will lead these actions to become a part of their everyday behavior in ways they won't even realize but will benefit from greatly.

As you no doubt realized in your reflection, good conversations can be challenging. The types of conversations you reflected on were likely in person, but did you consider asynchronous conversations? Conversations are even harder without synchronicity and depth. This form of communication is becoming increasingly common and includes text messages, tweets, and their many social media variations, emoji exchanges, and even email shorthand. Given that these are the types of conversations that many adolescents are having, you can see the importance of students being able to practice conversation skills. There is a necessity for real-time teaching and modeling in order to develop these skills with increased sophistication as students mature. More specifically, MCCs are meant to target Grades 5 through 12, recognizing that qualities of a genuine conversation may evolve throughout that developmental age span.

WHY ADOLESCENCE?

Human beings crave meaningful connection and want to feel heard, whether in person, by video, or through asynchronous exchange, and the adolescent population does not stray from that human desire. Erikson's developmental stages and more recent work by Damon and colleagues on the development of purpose provide a frame for understanding this need (Damon et al., 2003; Munley, 1975). As you may recall from your own higher education days, individuals from ages 12 to 18 are in the "Identity vs. Role Confusion" stage. During the transition from childhood to adulthood, individuals want to become more independent and begin to look at future relationships, family, education, and career paths to support the determination of who they truly want to be.

During this developmental stage, many adolescents' actions are attempts to answer the question, "Who am I?" and the question, "What can I become?" These are large, philosophical questions that are difficult for children to properly address and typically require a significant amount of unpacking. Another issue is that the answer to both of these questions suffers from social/historical baggage, including racism. Yet, young people are not seeking abstract answers but rather guidance for living their lives *now*, in a way that seems headed toward a meaningful future. This is where MCCs come along, with the goal of expanding young peoples' horizons, their sense of personal possibility, and piloting them on their journey of social and emotional development. All students deserve to see themselves as engaged citizens whose voices and views matter and who, by their engagement, can make a difference and change past historical trajectories. As noted in *Educational Leadership* (Krahenbuhl, 2020), "classroom conversations should be a refuge from our fast-paced, me-first culture" (p. 28). They help students pay attention to others around them and attend more deeply to what they are saying.

SEL skills and character are essential tools to help guide adolescents on this journey. Especially during the middle school years, every day can seem life-defining. Friendships seem to be made or lost forever; good or bad test scores or performance in the arts or sports bring alternative futures in and out of focus. Skills in perspective taking, empathy, self-awareness, problem-solving, and getting along with others in various groups situations are put into use over time. Adolescents want and need to communicate about what they are feeling. Every generation of adolescents speaks in a variety of unique ways, especially, now, with social media and text and video messages. The desire for connection expands beyond speaking because adolescents also want to know that what they say has been heard. That's what happens in a good conversation; you know if you have been understood; and if not, you can correct someone right on the spot, and then the conversation can improve and proceed.

It's from the perspective of genuine conversation that students come to understand the limits of the abbreviated forms of conversation that many people, especially adolescents, use today. Without that perspective, many young people's view of themselves and their future is at the mercy of how their social media communications are made and responded to. As we know too well, this can take the extreme form of making adolescents hypersensitive to cyberbullying—even to the point of anxiety, depression, or suicidality. In order to protect youth from such potentially harmful situations, the goal is to help each student establish a sense of purpose and positive self-esteem through foundational social-emotional skills and genuine connections, which are often established and sustained through good conversations.

HOW ARE CONVERSATIONAL SKILLS AND SEL CONNECTED?

For those of you who are familiar with SEL, a connection between SEL skills and genuine conversations may have started to register already. Although research has been studying SEL for years (Durlak et al., 2015), "SEL" has recently become the newest buzzword around schools. Educators now are increasingly recognizing the impact of SEL across many areas and the necessity of making time for such skill-building throughout all grades. While social and emotional skills, such as sharing, problem-solving, caring, and patience, are developed and understood based on modeling and practice in the home, children and adolescents spend much of their time in school. Just as reading cannot be reserved only for schools, social-emotional development, as well as character, cannot be reserved only for the home (Waangard et al., 2014). As we will show, MCCs provide an efficient vehicle for social-emotional and character development (SECD). First, however, it is important to provide clarity on buzzword terms as those who use these terms sometimes mean different things by them (Elias, 2013).

Explicitly defined, SEL is a "process through which children and adults acquire and effectively apply the knowledge, attitudes, and skills necessary to understand and manage emotions, set and achieve positive goals, feel and show empathy for others, establish and maintain positive relationships, and make responsible decisions" (Collaborative for Academic, Social, and Emotional Learning [CASEL], 2018). As the definition implies, SEL is incorporated in nearly every interaction that humans have and is an ongoing process throughout life. SEL is a prerequisite for individuals to have the capability to interact appropriately with others and regulate feelings and thoughts.

TABLE 1.1 ● CASEL's Five SEL Competencies (adapted from www.CASEL.org)

Self-Awareness	Refers to understanding one's own emotions, thoughts, and values and how they influence behavior across contexts. This includes capacities to recognize one's strengths and limitations with a well-grounded sense of confidence and purpose.
Self-Management	Includes the ability to manage one's emotions, thoughts, and behaviors effectively in different situations and to achieve goals and aspirations. This includes the capacities to delay gratification, manage stress, and feel motivation and agency to accomplish personal and collective goals.
Responsible Decision Making	Skills involved in making caring and constructive choices about personal behavior and social interactions across diverse situations. This includes the capacities to consider ethical standards and safety concerns, and to evaluate the benefits and consequences of various actions for personal, social, and collective well-being.
Relationship Skills	Refers to being able to establish and maintain healthy and supportive relationships and to effectively navigate settings with diverse individuals and groups. This includes the capacities to communicate clearly, listen actively, cooperate, work collaboratively to problem-solve and negotiate conflict constructively, navigate settings with differing social and cultural demands and opportunities, provide leadership, and seek or offer help when needed.
Social Awareness	Includes the ability to understand the perspectives of and empathize with others, including those from diverse backgrounds, cultures, and contexts. This includes the capacities to feel compassion for others, understand broader historical and social norms for behavior in different settings, and recognize family, school, and community resources and supports.

CASEL has delineated five basic competencies that comprise SEL skills: self-awareness, self-management, responsible decision-making, social awareness, and relationship skills (see Table 1.1). These skills reflect what children need for success in school and life: they are going to have to be ethical problem solvers, understand their feelings and those of others, be able to take the perspective of diverse individuals and empathize with them, engage in nonviolent conflict resolution, and they will need to work effectively with people in groups, in both leadership and contributor roles. In CASEL's most recent formulation, SEL is also essential for the reduction of biases of all kinds, including racism, and the promotion of equity grounded in compassion for others, particularly those different from oneself.

SECD is defined as "the capacity to recognize and manage emotions, solve problems effectively, take others' perspectives, and establish positive, empathic relationships with others—competencies that are essential for the development of all students" (Rutgers SECD Lab, 2018). What the SECD perspective adds is a recognition that skills need to be directed toward virtuous ends. So, SECD emphasizes students developing a sense of positive purpose and associated virtues, such as optimism, gratitude, and forgiveness. For adolescents in particular, being associated with making constructive contributions to others plays an important role in their identity development, and therefore in the motivation to learn and improve SEL skills. For simplicity sake, when SEL is used hereafter in the book, the authors are referring to their brand of SEL, which is SECD.

Each year, teachers around the world search for ways to help establish rapport and ensure their students feel connected to the classroom community. SEL skills are essential for this to happen positively and for supporting students' social adjustment, enhancing civic participation, and improving teacher–student relationships (Taylor et al., 2017; Weissberg, 2019). Students who are effectively taught social-emotional skills, on both an intrapersonal and an interpersonal level, are more positively adjusted to their schools, including those in marginalized groups (CASEL, 2013, 2015; Domitrovich et al., 2017). Not every school is using an SEL curriculum; even when they are used, they often are not sufficient to ensure these skills will be internalized and generalized to all aspects of students' lives. That's why MCCs were developed, as a way to exercise your students' SEL muscles. Put forth a small investment of time, daily or as often as you can, repeated over multiple years, and you have provided quite a meaningful and long-lasting repertoire of skills.

SEL skills are needed for youth to find their voice and become active members of society. Even as adults, you can likely think of a group of friends and/or family members where "sensitive topics" such as politics, racial injustice, or gender equality are not to be spoken about. Why is that? It seems simple for adults to generally get along with each other and help others, but an increasingly polarized society encourages avoidance of conversation, rather than making efforts toward continued practice with perspective taking, empathy, problem-solving, and embracing diversity. Therefore, the vulnerability and potential disagreement with which many people are not comfortable stops many adults from engaging in important conversations. The reality is these conversations must be had, both now and throughout our future.

Similar to how these conversations must be had in adulthood, MCCs allow for students to make continued efforts toward understanding and equity. The students will get better at them over time, with your guidance. Some catch on faster than others, but just about anyone can learn to participate with patient support and encouragement from you and other students. Elias and Nayman (2019), in a civic participation program called "Students Taking Action Together (STAT)," have seen the benefits for students when they are given structured opportunities to identify an issue within their school/community, utilize a structured problem-solving model, create a plan, and carry out their change. With such a structure, students come to believe that their voices matter and that they have the potential to make a productive, collaborative impact. Not only does SEL support positive development, but the preventive nature of SEL can also decrease behavior incidents, reduce emotional deficits linked to mental health concerns like depression, increase resilience to adverse childhood experiences, and decrease substance abuse.

 ## WHAT ARE MCCS?

By this point, you might be saying, "This sounds great, but what exactly is a Morning Classroom Conversation?" As we have seen through extensive research and shared practice around Morning Meeting, the transition from the home to school environment can be difficult for our students (Kriete & Davis, 2014). Although much existing research targets elementary-aged students, entry into school may be even harder for middle school and high school students. This is amplified in times of crisis or in traumatic contexts. If you ask most people, "Would you go back to middle school?" most would quickly respond, "No," and there is a reason for that. Even at its smoothest, adolescent development poses significant challenges; in particular, the desire for connectedness is strong but must be balanced off against fears about social judgment. Further more, students will vary in the extent to which they want to acknowledge or express this tension. In an effort to address these underlying needs, MCCs facilitate classroom or group-based conversations for youth to develop a strong character both socially and emotionally.

The MCCs are meant to be a daily 10- to 15-minute conversation to start the school day, which allows the opportunity for middle school and high school students to transition from the outside world to the academic day. The length of the conversations is important, as anything too much shorter than 10 minutes may limit the depth of the discussion and anything much longer than 15 minutes may lead the students to become restless and lose interest in the topic being discussed. The potency of MCCs comes from their frequency, not from their duration on any given day.

In pilot MCCs, the conversations were often occurring during homeroom or an advisory period. As this could be considered underutilized time, fostering connection, conversation, and skill development are fruitful. We also understand that homeroom/advisory periods do not exist in all schools, so there are alternative implementation models explored further in Chapter 6.

MCCs can be led by you, the reader, who is likely a teacher, psychologist, social worker, master teacher, out-of-school group leader, school counselor, or others with ongoing responsibility for leading small or large groups of youth. "Conversation Leader" is the term used throughout this book for those who are guiding conversations, and the chapters that follow provide you with the preparation and materials required to engage in this role. The materials in this book will enable you to lead MCCs with your students and, in our final chapter, also assist you in how to prepare ways to introduce MCCs to colleagues via workshops, professional development, and collaborating with colleagues who have seen you put MCCs into practice and want to follow in your footsteps. For you (and for others who will engage in MCCs), introspection and self-awareness are imperative first steps in readiness, similar to the earlier part of the chapter when you reflected on a good conversation in your life. By taking these steps, you are better able to create a safe and supportive environment, what is called the "brave space," for your students to start their day.

If students know that their classroom always will be a place where their views are welcomed, their opinions respected, and perspectives expanded, they are much more likely to arrive ready to learn and more effectively engage in the classroom community (Vieno et al., 2004). Adolescents look forward to this time; sometimes it is like an oasis in a desert. Therefore, when Conversation Leaders start each day by opening the floor with a simple MCC prompt, you help students manage some of the strong feelings they are bringing in from home or about the prospects for the school day. Middle and high school students tend to generally focus on the self, so being given a voice at the outset of their day is appreciated. Then, they will be better prepared for the tasks of the learning day ahead.

THE UNDERLYING STRUCTURE OF MCCS

There are four major dimensions that comprise the framework for MCCs: skills, virtues, themes, and development. Through MCCs, youth will have an opportunity to exercise their SEL and conversation muscles together by strengthening *skills* such as emotion regulation, empathy, communication, and social problem-solving. Additionally, there are targeted *virtues*, such as constructive creativity and optimistic future-mindedness, in these conversations that intentionally connect to what is known about a youth working to establish their identity and sense of purpose.

In addition to virtues and skills that are necessary to support adolescent development, there are various *themes* throughout the school year that are generalizable to most schools (e.g., September, "Why are we here?"). These "themes" also can be adaptable to current issues within the class or school. Last, there is the *development* and expansion of the focus of students' conversations and concerns over time. Students are asked to think in terms of what is needed for them to create a *Better Me–Better School–Better World* as a focus for application of their skills and virtues. This developmental approach can be used to create a non-duplicative series of MCCs over a three-year period (if you are able to work with students over an extended time frame or if you are coordinating MCCs with colleagues who will conduct conversations with the same group of students over three years). Of course, you also can address one or more of the developmental stages within a single year. As you would expect, the more students are exposed to all three developmental stages, the more MCCs can deepen students' sense of purpose related to civic participation and social action. These four dimensions are further explored in Chapter 2.

WHAT CAN YOU EXPECT FROM MCCS?

Pilot work in six schools yielded considerable feedback that was continuously used to improve the MCC structure and prompts. When surveyed about MCCs, one teacher's response captured it best: "Morning conversations were great."

Consultants reviewing feedback from meetings with teachers carrying out MCCs in pilot schools over the course of a year reported no negative feedback. Other feedback indicated that MCCs were used as a stimulus for journal writing, were valuable as a way to begin group counseling sessions, and led to fruitful discussions of culturally sensitive topics. Teachers also said that while they sometimes did not have time to complete their formal SEL lessons due to competing demands, it was not difficult to make time for MCCs. In this way, MCCs provide a consistent and ongoing thread for SEL skill and virtue development, regardless of what other formal SEL or character programming might be in place.

In Appendix D, you will find tools that allow for Conversation Leader and student self-tracking on the elements of good conversations mentioned earlier and on the development of SEL skills. In addition, a tool also is provided to help Conversation Leaders monitor progress toward the intended outcomes of MCCs, especially when done daily over the course of year and when students can experience them for multiple years in the *Better Me–Better School–Better World* developmental sequence. These outcomes are summarized in Table 1.2.

TABLE 1.2 ● MCC Outcomes

Students in my class/group get along well with one another.
Students work well together in groups.
Students are more willing to share during academic lessons.
Students are level-headed with regard to how they speak or act and rarely overreact.
Students appear to have more confidence when speaking to the class.
Students engage in productive conversations with their class/groupmates.
Students engage in productive conversations with me.
Students are respectful of class/groupmates opinions, even when they disagree.
Students are receptive to feedback about their ideas and communication style.
Students appear to be optimistic and have a growth mindset.
Students are willing to be generous to and forgiving of classmates.
Students are curious and creative and willing to "think out of the box."
Students have a clear sense of responsibility as relates to school.
Students tend to persist in problem-solving, rather than getting thrown off by roadblocks.
Students appear to have a sense of positive purpose and a good moral compass.

THE CHANGING CLASSROOM ...

This book would not be complete if it was not noted that, during its creation, the nature of the classroom has been challenged by various societal factors, such as the recent COVID-19 pandemic, the growing awareness of disparities and bias, the increased presence of social media and online learning, and concerns about the lack of civic engagement and civil discourse. In response to the pandemic, some classrooms maintain social distancing, some have barriers between desks, and some are conducted in a remote environment. Some meet only on certain days of the week, and some have strict directions about where, when, and how students can move around in and out of the classroom. Some students experience various combinations of these. Even when classrooms are attempting to go "back to normal," they do so with a heightened sense of inequitable and discriminatory practices, polarized views on many issues, and the knowledge that students will still spend inordinate amounts of time in front of screens.

SEL has gained significant attention during this time as schools consider how to continue social connection during remote learning, ways to integrate students back to school, best practices for maintaining a trauma-informed approach, ways to confront and counter racism, and, of course, the continued concern with academic proficiency and reducing disparities in achievement. SEL skills are at the heart of redressing all these issues because they all are interpersonal in nature and require addressing strong emotions, taking many perspectives, and solving numerous problems. If students are equipped with the SEL skills to help them identify social cues and be more careful with their inferencing, they are more likely to develop a responsible sense of purpose both online and in person. This book is intended to provide you with the guidance to use MCCs to accomplish these goals, and as questions arise, Table 1.3 can direct you where to find the answer!

TABLE 1.3 ● MCC Question and Answer Guide

WHAT YOU MIGHT BE WONDERING	WHERE YOU CAN FIND IT
How does the MCC framework help youth?	Chapter 2
Can my school pick skills, virtues, and themes that relate to our population?	Chapter 2
How do I go about getting started with getting MCC off the ground in my classroom/group?	Chapter 3
Do I need to create the MCC prompts or do you provide them to me?	Chapter 3
What is a brave space?	Chapter 3
Do I need to do practice conversations before engaging in MCCs?	Chapter 4
What if some of my students have had MCCs in the past but others have never done an MCC?	Chapter 4
What if the homeroom period is already filled with other activities and I want to engage in this during my English classes?	Chapter 5
What if I start MCCs and my students aren't engaged?	Chapter 5
How do I prevent MCCs from taking up academic and core content time?	Chapter 5
What if I am a school counselor and I don't have a homeroom, is there another format to engage students in these conversations?	Chapter 6
What if I can't do MCCs every day with my group?	Chapter 6
Can MCCs be done in other contexts outside of a classroom?	Chapter 6
How do I differentiate for the unique needs within my classroom?	Chapter 7
How do MCCs progress over the years?	Chapter 8
How do I adapt MCC prompts to include more than one developmental stage in a single year?	Chapter 8
Can one Conversation Leader do this or does a whole school need to buy in?	Chapter 9
What if I am an administrator/lead teacher and want support in how to get my Conversation Leaders to buy in?	Chapter 9

Chapter Wrap-Up

Understanding the research and motivation behind the MCC program is crucial in creating genuine investment and commitment with students and Conversation Leaders. We began by revisiting the lost art of conversation. Looking at what worked best and not so well in past conversations helped illustrate the importance of SEL skills in carrying out those conversations. For adolescents, being able to listen to classmates and not just worry about what they want to say and what others will think about them is the start of developing their sense of positive purpose. In school, at home, in the community, and as part of the wider world, our students need to learn to speak with one another using empathy and fostering connection. To address this need, Morning Classroom Conversations were introduced as daily 10- to 15-minute conversations for students, Grades 5 through 12, implemented by teachers, school mental health professionals, or others with the ongoing responsibility of a group of adolescents. The goal of MCCs is to accomplish building a closer, more productive, inclusive, and caring classroom environment while also further developing students' SEL skills, character, sense of purpose, and overall wellness.

Reflective Conversations for Growth

At the end of each chapter, there are a series of questions to help you reflect on the chapter you just read. This "Reflective Conversations for Growth" is imperative to your development as an MCC Conversation Leader because it will allow you to have something similar to an MCC with yourself, your colleagues, and/or an SEL expert. As a Conversation Leader, you will want to explore the steps you might need to effectively prepare for MCCs. By doing so, you will deepen your learning and readiness and have the opportunity to think about how best to navigate your MCCs within the school, what support might be needed among colleagues, and the community resources that could help you.

These conversations are organized into the following sections: (a) Action Steps/ Priorities, (b) Adaptations, (c) Challenges, and (d) Questions. With one or two questions or points to consider for each of these areas and consistent usage of these subheadings throughout all Reflective Conversations for Growth, the reader is allowed an opportunity to contemplate on chapter content in an intentional, organized way.

(Continued)

The Action Steps/Priorities questions are meant to help the reader reflect on the content of the chapter to determine what should be included within their action plan. By considering priorities, the many elements embedded into the chapter can be organized into an applicable list of what matters most within their school. In addition to the Action Steps, we understand that MCCs will be adjusted and modified for the unique needs of each population. Therefore, the second set of questions explores Adaptations that will need to be made in order to make the MCCs suitable. Next, there is a set of questions related to Challenges. Typically, when exploring content, a reader is able to quickly consider anticipated obstacles within their school. Using the Reflective Conversations for Growth, the reader is able to anticipate these challenges and problem solve, accordingly.

At the end of each "Reflective Conversation for Growth," you will be asked to consider seeking answers to questions that remain. Some questions and/or comments are encouraged to be submitted to the Social-Emotional Learning Alliance for the United States (www.SEL4US.org), and/or your state SEL4US affiliate to learn more about what is happening locally and nationally in SEL that might help you better bring MCCs to your students. SEL4US is an organization dedicated to increasing awareness of SEL and supporting high-quality and equitable implementation of SEL-related efforts. At the state and community level, SEL4US makes teachers, administrators, and all community members aware of the best ways to develop social-emotional competence among our youth. Additionally, there is sometimes a suggestion at the end of each chapter for readers to email the authors at morningclassroomconversations@gmail.com with any question specific to MCCs that cannot be answered by their administration or colleagues. The questions and answers will then be posted to the MCC website, resources.corwin.com/MorningClassroomConversations. By consulting with those in nationally and locally recognized organizations, as well as the authors when necessary, the reader will be better able to explore the content of the chapter in a unique way and consider what is working in other locations. So let's give it a try ...

Now that you have seen the basic rationale for MCCs and why the art of conversation is so important to the development of youth civil discourse, SEL development and more, reflect on/write down the following and commit to taking the appropriate follow-up actions in order to continue to learn and grow as a Conversation Leader.

ACTION STEPS/PRIORITIES

List one thing you learned or gained from this chapter.

_____

_____

_____

ADAPTATIONS

Note one thought about how the topics within this chapter will need to be adapted within your classroom.

_____

_____

_____

CHALLENGES

Write about one difficulty that you foresee within your setting.

_____

_____

_____

QUESTIONS

Note the question that you still have. What do you want to learn more about? Where will you find this information?

_____

_____

_____

CHAPTER 2

Morning Classroom Conversations Instructional Framework

R ecent firsthand work by the MCC program developers has provided a fresh perspective on what students respond to and what their current school climate often lacks, with regard to fostering social and emotional growth. Foremost is the need for classrooms to provide explicit opportunities for synergistic, frequent conversations that give students a voice. These types of classroom-based conversations also serve as a reinforcement for social-emotional learning (SEL)–related lessons that may already be integrated into a school's curriculum and school environment. This need for synergy, student expression, and reinforcement of social and emotional growth is what inspired Morning Classroom Conversations (MCCs) and the framework behind it. A systematic series of MCC prompts provide a guide for how teachers and other school staff can convey school-wide themes, skills, and virtues to all students in a safe and approachable way. MCCs are designed specifically for secondary students (i.e., those in Grades 5–12) and will allow an opportunity for youth to engage in meaningful SEL-based conversations to start their school day.

As introduced in Chapter 1, there are four main dimensions in the MCC framework: skills, virtues, themes, and development, all with the unifying theme of Positive Purpose. This chapter will explore the MCC framework in greater detail by discussing each of these dimensions in depth, and, at the end, provide and discuss a full sample month of MCCs. Conversation Leaders (those that facilitate the MCCs such as teachers, psychologists, social workers, master teachers, out-of-school group leaders, etc.) may use the template in Figure 2.1 to create a visual overview of what their year will look like with MCCs. The chart in Figure 2.1 describes the framework that has been used effectively and will be the source of the examples provided in this book. Please consider this chart as a model framework and modify as you wish to create your own Year-Long Themes, Virtues, and Skills chart that best suits your classroom and school context. Themes, while linked to the flow of the school year, are best honed to fit your local concerns, and local themes can be *added to* or *integrated with* the flow that is outlined in Figure 2.1.

 DIMENSION 1: MCC SKILLS

In order for an individual to be successful in relationships, careers, and daily life, one must have, at minimum, the following skills: emotion regulation, communication, empathy and perspective taking, and social problem-solving. These will look familiar as SEL skills. While interactions in and out of school require all SEL skills, it is instructionally wise to focus on certain key skills to which the others are linked.

Emotion Regulation. Emotion regulation, as you may have found, is a popular term in education today. This refers to one's ability to have optimal awareness and control over their emotions, when they are felt, and how they are expressed. Included in this are both positive and negative emotions. It is particularly salient when discussing emotions such as anxiety, frustration, anger, sadness, or excitement,

FIGURE 2.1 ● Year-Long Themes, Virtues, and Skills Chart

Morning Classroom Conversations

Monthly Themes, Virtues and Skills

POSITIVE PURPOSE

 Supporting Virtues

1. Constructive Creativity
2. Helpful Generosity
3. Optimistic Future-Mindedness
4. Responsible Diligence
5. Compassionate Forgiveness
   and Gratitude

Supporting Skills

1. Emotional Regulation
2. Communication
3. Empathy and Perspective Taking
4. Social Problem-Solving

Month	Theme	Virtue	Skills
November	Making Ourselves, School and World Better	Constructive Creativity	Communication and Social Problem-Solving
December	Giving Back to Ourselves, School and World	Helpful Generosity	Communication and Social Problem-Solving
January	Planning for the Future	Optimistic Future-Mindedness	Empathy and Perspective Taking; Social Problem-Solving
February	Showing Resilience and Overcoming Obstacles	Responsible Diligence	Emotion Regulation; Social Problem-Solving
March	Appreciating Ourselves, Our School and the World	Compassionate Gratitude	Communication; Empathy and Perspective Taking
April	Connecting with Others and Being a Leader	Compassionate Forgiveness	Emotion Regulation; Empathy and Perspective Taking
May	Looking Forward: Next Steps on the Journey	Positive Purpose	Communication and Social Problem-Solving
June	Looking Back: What Have I Accomplished? What Have I Learned?	All Virtues Summary	All Skills Integrated

and how emotional regulation can be used to control reactions to certain situations that may incite a high level of these emotions. Classrooms can't function when kids are hostile, dejected, or incredibly giddy. This skill is especially important with adolescents, given their stage of development and its effects on their hormone levels and heightened sensitivity to their environment and their emotions.

Some SEL advocates have expressed concern that SEL can be used as an instrument of emotional repression (Simmons, 2019). The point of building students' emotion regulation skills is not to make them docile and compliant. Emotion regulation does not mean "doing what adults tell you to do." Emotion regulation means that students are able to modify their own emotions to be appropriate to situations they are in, as they perceive them. Biologically, it's about students controlling their amygdala reactions versus having their amygdala reactions control them. It means being better able to resist provocations and to handle difficult situations thoughtfully. As fostered by MCCs, emotion regulation is essential for civil discourse and effective social action.

Communication. Communication is not a single skill but a combination of many skills, skills that are necessary to carry messages to the world. If students have great ideas and can't express them, few if anyone will know about these ideas. If strong emotions are not able to be managed, the ability to send a message in a way that clearly conveys intentions or plans can be impaired. Communication can get complicated and multifaceted, and without explicit skill building in communication, the quality of exchanges that students have with one another and with the adults in their lives will not be as positive and fruitful as they could be.

Communication is defined as a process by which information is exchanged between individuals through a common system of symbols, signs, or behavior, and it is necessary in order to successfully navigate through daily life. Communication is inherently at the forefront of the MCC skills, because it is practiced every day by listening and responding to the conversations that transpire from the daily prompts. However, similar to the other focal SEL skills, MCCs also address communication explicitly in certain skill-driven prompts so that students can discuss the many different methods of communication that have arisen in recent years (best denoted by various and ever-evolving social media), potential unknown factors that impact communication, and how other skills such as empathy and emotion regulation relate to improving communication skills.

Empathy and Perspective Taking. What is referred to in Western religion as the Golden Rule—"Do unto others as you would have others do unto you"—is an exemplification of the importance of taking others' perspective and having empathy. It turns out that in virtually all of the world's major religions, there is an equivalent statement that is regarded as foundational (Templeton, 2002). The connection of empathy and perspective taking reflects the necessity of combining both the heart and the head in understanding and relating to others.

Let's take a closer look, to see why these skills are explicitly taught in various prompts throughout the daily MCCs. Empathy and perspective taking refer to the ability to understand and vicariously experience the feelings, thoughts, and behaviors of another. It requires one to not *assume* how others are feeling but rather *seek out cues* to how they might be feeling. It requires getting into the shoes of the other person to see circumstances as he or she might be seeing them, rather than looking at the situation exclusively introspectively. No doubt, this is calling forth current emphases on the way racial bias or blindness impacts everyday interactions for many. It's not easy getting into the shoes of someone whose shoes you may never have seen. It's not possible to experience every other culture and every other context, but it is also not necessary. Human brains have been hardwired to pick up cues about circumstances that are unfamiliar or uncomfortable. That hardwiring tends to be protective and cautious and that makes evolutionary sense. But the frontal lobe, in combination with emotion regulation, makes it possible to think and not always instantly react. It allows someone to consider, in an instant, "What else could this be?" Students require that kind of empathy and perspective every day, to better understand the thoughts, feelings, and actions of others; this can improve communication and, in turn, improve social interaction.

Social Problem-Solving. MCCs explicitly address the social-emotional skill of problem-solving. Anytime there is a dilemma in a social situation, students should be capable of choosing the right skill or combination of skills from their SEL toolbox to resolve the situation and improve the outcome for all involved. For this to happen most effectively, adolescents benefit from having a strategy they can turn to in these situations.

If you reflect on your own experiences in school, where you encounter many problems every day with students, parents, and colleagues, you likely will notice that when you have a strategy to deal with them, they are less stressful to handle. And the outcomes usually are better. But when every situation is responded to as if it never happened before, not only are the same mistakes often made over and over, but it's also exhausting and frustrating. Sometimes, by helping students develop social problem-solving strategies during MCCs, it can be easier to better attend to and improve your own strategies!

This skill will be reviewed by taking a sample prompt that is provided later in this book. Consider asking students, as a whole class, "The student next to you in class is trying to copy your paper during a test. What should you do?" This prompt creates an opportunity for students to explore their feelings about the situation and weigh the costs and benefits of potential choices of action and putting their other MCC skills to best use. It also serves as a gauge for you about students' problem-solving skills and moral compass. As they respond, you can highlight the SEL in their response. For example, a student may use empathy by suggesting a strategy that involves speaking to that student after class and encouraging them to be truthful to the teacher in hopes of getting the academic assistance they may need. Alternatively, a student may advocate using emotion regulation by avoiding getting upset and frustrated in the moment and instead speaking in a calm fashion. If a student were to say, "Stand up and tell the teacher what that student is doing and to stop it," a response that facilitates problem-solving would be to ask, "What would all the consequences of doing that be?" and "How else might the situation be handled, using empathy and perspective taking as a guide?"

All the skills emphasized in MCCs together create the tools necessary for students to effectively engage socially both within their classrooms and outside of the classroom in their daily interactions. By practicing conversations involving situations that could become challenging, negative, or unproductive, students can instead create more positive outcomes, build stronger relationships, and improve their overall well-being. Most important, these skills set the foundation for the next important dimension of MCCs, the virtues.

 ## DIMENSION 2: MCC VIRTUES

As you will notice in the template provided earlier in Figure 2.1, the core virtues within MCCs include constructive creativity, helpful generosity, optimistic future-mindedness, responsible diligence, compassionate gratitude and forgiveness, and positive purpose. Of these, positive purpose is superordinate. It fits with the key questions that adolescents are trying to answer: "Who am I? What can I become?" While it is the rare youth that knows their life purpose in adolescence—particular early adolescence—it is both common and desirable that adolescents "try on" different purposes for varying lengths of time. Research suggests that when youth have a sense of purpose, they are better able to function as learners, classmates, and friends (Malin, 2018).

Positive purpose is affected by a set of supportive virtues. These virtues have been identified as helping adolescents move forward, particularly in trauma-informed contexts (which now seem ubiquitous), toward the development of their sense of positive purpose (Hatchimonji et al., 2017, 2019; Malin, 2018). Trauma, particularly chronic trauma such as poverty, racism, or early loss or severe illness of a parent, functionally limits an individuals' sense of who they are and what they can become. Often, young people can get caught up in resentful demoralization, revenge, hopelessness, or internalized marginalization. The virtues that will be discussed, and that MCCs are particularly designed to exercise, are necessary for building a virtuous cycle from a vicious cycle of self-fulfilling negative prophecy. To have effective conversations with others, one must feel that one has something to bring to the encounter and that one can benefit as well as contribute. Adolescents need these virtues to continue to engage in genuine exchange.

Helpful Generosity. Helpful generosity as a virtue means, in essence, that no matter what my life difficulties are, no matter what challenges loom, I have something to contribute. The intangible and intrinsic rewards of helpful generosity—from holding doors for others, sitting next to isolated classmates, helping someone who looks confused, being a caring friend, helping harmonize groups one is part of in school or out—can encourage a sense of positive purpose in the helping professions. Particularly for students who are used to being "remediated," the idea that they have something to give to others is a powerful counternarrative to abject failure. Generosity also requires one to be perceptive of others' needs and feelings. In MCCs, students are encouraged to strive for and work toward genuine understanding of others and to see themselves as being sources of help, including for school and community problems. Civic engagement and positive social action flow from having Helpful Generosity as a personal virtue.

Optimistic Future-Mindedness. Why have a conversation if you don't believe it can accomplish anything, or that you don't have anything worth saying? Having students exercise this virtue helps them to believe things can be improved and that they can have an active role in that improvement. This is complemented by fostering a growth mindset, or the belief that abilities, situations, and environments can be improved through hard work and dedication, as well as intrinsic motivation, the inner drive to pursue an activity due to genuine interest, and enjoyment. This does not come easily to students who have experienced ongoing trauma, who have been saddled with attending "failing schools," and who themselves have been failed by teachers, parents, educators, and/or other human services professionals whose job it was to help them. That's why MCCs require repetition over the course of a year and over the course of three years. Establishing positive virtues as self-habits takes time and practice. The result: students adopt a kind of future-mindedness that is optimistic in order to maintain the belief and the motivation to continuously improve the possibility of a Positive Purpose in their future.

Constructive Creativity. Constructive creativity encourages genuine exchange by allowing students to think outside of the box regarding ongoing social issues, peer conflicts, relationship building, and self-expression. This virtue also fosters openness to other thoughts, feelings, and beliefs. Creativity is most aligned with positive purpose when it is constructive because it specifies that creativity should be utilized to constantly improve one's self, their relationships, and their larger communities. With constructive creativity, students are better able to see a pathway to positive purpose despite social stigma, pressure, or bias against pursuing those pathways. And because adolescents will inevitably encounter problems along the way to their positive purpose, having an attitude of constructive creativity will help them move forward with optimism.

Responsible Diligence. Responsible diligence is a close cousin of social problem-solving. In a sense, it's the virtue that benefits from and spurs on a problem-solving mindset. In order to have genuine exchange, students must begin to understand that those around them will not always, perhaps not usually, be in agreement with their views. This is inevitable and not necessarily a negative. The conversation will continue regardless, because of the belief that persisting in the process of exchange can lead to a mutual understanding. As students pursue social action, they will find ever-increasing obstacles to their ideas. They cannot allow themselves to be deterred by this. They need responsible diligence to persist constructively. During MCCs, students get practice in handling disagreements, focusing their conversations on seeking understanding and mutual problem-solving, rather than just expressing one's viewpoint and expecting agreement. They come to learn that civil conversations and civic engagement will take both a considerable amount of diligence as well as responsibility, but are well worth it!

Compassionate Forgiveness and Gratitude. The final set of virtues emphasized in MCCs is compassionate forgiveness and gratitude. Research into these areas has increased dramatically and has shown clear benefits to both young people and adults (Chiaramello et al., 2008; Dutro & Bien, 2014). The inability to forgive—seen most familiarly in holding grudges—has far more negative effects on the "offended" party than the alleged perpetrator. For youth in trauma-beset contexts, there is often resentment and forgiveness might be seen as weak. However, it is a virtue that, left uncultivated, can effectively cut off a path to positive purpose.

Relatedly, even (and sometimes especially) among those who have the fewest material possessions and advantages, gratitude for what one does have can be a force for good in one's life. (Some might view this as an example of fostering docility and submission; however, forgiveness exists alongside the other virtues—solutions to social problems fueled by envy, hatred, and revenge rarely have good long-term outcomes.) It is not unusual for an "attitude of gratitude" to spur helpful generosity and optimistic future-mindedness, creating a pathway toward positive purpose. March 30, 2020 was the first Worldwide Day of Gratitude (https://www .younison.org/leanonus) and an extraordinary array of materials to promote this virtue was collected for ongoing use. This is one of many ways that the essential role of gratitude has been recognized.

Exercising compassionate forgiveness and gratitude in MCCs teaches students the benefits and appropriateness of feeling care and compassion toward their peers—much as they would want peers to feel the same toward themselves. It is important to show compassion and support by respecting and valuing differing viewpoints, even in situations where there is a disagreement or someone may otherwise become upset or frustrated. This also can apply to the actions of others, meaning that when someone does something that someone else dislikes or that has a negative impact, care and compassion must be used in order to have a better understanding of the actions of others and move forward with a more positive viewpoint. Adolescence is a good time to start to learn that it is all right to be upset about someone's actions but that they need not reject that person altogether or fail to see what is good about them.

Each month throughout the school year will be dedicated to one or more of the virtues described earlier, with the exception of September and October (or the first and second months of the school year), which is left as a time for teachers and students to acclimate to the new school year. As each virtue is learned, understood, and practiced, the subsequent virtues will then build on and often show strong links to one another. MCCs are intentionally formatted with an understanding that skills create the foundation for exercising virtues, and virtues are linked together to help students find their positive purpose.

 ## DIMENSION 3: MCC MONTHLY THEMES

Another component of MCCs that ties in closely with both skills and virtues is monthly themes. MCCs include various themes that emerge throughout the year that are generalizable to most schools (e.g., January/Month Three: Planning for the future; June: Looking back: What have I accomplished? What have I learned?). Please refer to the one-page MCC summary (Figure 2.1) to review the full list of monthly themes in MCCs.

As you approach this section of the chapter, you may ask yourself, why are themes necessary when skills and virtues are already in place for each month? The answer is both simple and complex. Simply put, the MCC themes work in connection with the virtues and skills to foster positive purpose, which is the overarching theme and overall goal for full participation in the MCC structure. Possessing positive purpose means that a student has found their drive to achieve and discovered how they can make a positive impact on the world around them. Themes are a kind of glue that holds skills and virtues together in the life of a student, a classroom, and a school.

Indeed, students all spend many days engaged in schooling (whether in person or virtually), beginning toward the end of summer, proceeding through fall and winter, and culminating at the tail end of spring or perhaps the earliest days of summer. There is a flow to these days, to how school years unfold, and students think about this. (So do staff, often being excited about the start of the year, dreading standardized testing in the spring, and exhaustedly looking forward to the end of the year!) Therefore, focusing prompts around these monthly themes often taps into what is on students' minds and helps create conversations that assist students in their journey through self-exploration.

Conversation Leaders also should keep in mind that these themes will provide tremendous synergy with any social-emotional and character development program or other similar approach your school is already using or will choose to take on. For example, if there is a specific evidence-based curriculum, such as the Second Step program, or educational approach, such as trauma-informed teaching, that your school has implemented, you can and should intertwine these approaches by regularly referencing them. As a Conversation Leader, you can connect themes related to these approaches into your MCCs and at other times throughout the school day and in various contexts. The more generalized and connected the themes, virtues, and skills become, the more cohesive they become to the overall educational experience, and the more likely your school and your students are to successfully retain and use what they are learning.

In addition to strengthening existing SEL strategies and programs, if a specific issue were to arise in the classroom and/or school, the "theme" structure is adaptable to target these areas. For instance, if there is a problem with a rise in bullying in a middle school, this could be a targeted theme for that schools' MCCs for an appropriate period, by incorporating complementary skills such as social problem-solving, virtues such as compassionate forgiveness and gratitude, or themes such as connecting with others and being a leader. Schools in New Jersey recognize October as "anti-bullying month," complemented by a week in that month designated as the Week of Respect. Creating a theme in October around this context certainly would make sense for New Jersey schools. The MCC themes that have been presented are meant to be general enough to easily adapt to each school-specific climate and culture needs.

DIMENSION 4: MCC THREE-YEAR DEVELOPMENTAL PROGRESSION

As a teacher, administrator, support staff, or a member of the school community, you are well aware of noticeable differences in students as they develop through adolescence. The common trends of social and emotional development must be considered when implementing MCCs and other social-emotional character development (SECD) programs. In an effort to correlate with the increase in sophistication and maturity across grade levels, the MCC model utilizes a three-year *Better Me–Better School–Better World* developmental framework. With this framework, it is not necessary to formulate different questions and topics for every grade level; rather, the questions are adapted to be focused on their application and relevance to the self, the school community, and then the wider world, as students' progress in their development.

The *Better Me–Better School–Better World* framework, as its name suggests, targets a different set of goals each year. The *Better Me* framework has students focus on improving themselves, exploring their interests and beliefs, and reflecting on their own actions. The *Better School* framework encourages students to continue to apply the skills and virtues to themselves and expand their thinking to apply those skills to their school community, whether it be their classroom, their school, or school-related events in their town. Last, the *Better World* framework further challenges students to think about their influence on larger communities around them, including their municipality, their state, their country, or the world. Each year in this framework is meant to build upon the previous year and further challenge students' thinking and actions.

The progression might look like Table 2.1 for February/Month Four.

By referring to the same themes across grade levels, students can revisit past topics and expand their conversations from a more advanced social and emotional lens. In

TABLE 2.1 ● MCC Theme: Showing Resilience and Overcoming Obstacles

Year 1—*Better Me*	Students explore how to express themselves, to learn from their mistakes, and to be self-aware, among other skills.
Year 2—*Better School*	Students discuss how to work well with others even in the face of social challenges and to be aware of how their thoughts and actions impact others around them.
Year 3—*Better World*	Students discuss topics such as how certain mindsets can impact larger communities, how to seek out opportunities to share their views about social issues with others and take on leadership roles, and how to show appreciation and support for community members, first responders, and political leaders, etc.

addition, students' sense of positive purpose is expanded as they widen their horizons. For more examples of what this will look like in action, you can visit Chapter 8.

PUTTING IT ALL TOGETHER: WHAT MCCS LOOK LIKE OVER THE COURSE OF A MONTH

The background information presented thus far provides you with an understanding of the evidence-based foundation for MCCs. Now, it's time to take a look at what MCCs look like in practice, starting with a sample of MCCs carried out daily over the course of a month. There are other formats to use if daily MCCs seem too challenging, and these are presented later. However, it's best to start with the most basic program structure.

SAMPLE DAILY MCC STRUCTURE

The sample calendar in Table 2.2 demonstrates at a glance one month of suggested daily prompts. As MCCs are meant to follow a daily structure, each month is divided up into four weeks, with five prompts per week, depending on the typical number of school days in any given month. These twenty prompts shown in Table 2.2 are adaptable to a calendar format and can be utilized in part or in whole by Conversation Leaders. The chart provides the Year 1—*Better Me* structure for the month of January/Month Three, with the theme of Planning for the Future. We use the

TABLE 2.2 ● January/Month Three (Year 1—*Better Me*): Planning for the Future

	MONDAY	TUESDAY	WEDNESDAY	THURSDAY	FRIDAY
Week 1	A new student just arrived at your school. What do you think it feels like to be living in a new place with all new people? Has this happened to you? (Skill: Empathy)	What is one action you can take in your school now that will help prepare you for your dream job of the future? (Theme: Planning for the Future)	What is it like to work in a group where others do not communicate effectively to solve a problem? (Skill: Social Problem-Solving)	How can you nonverbally demonstrate that you are actively listening to your peers? (Skill: Empathy)	Not every moment in our lives is going to go well but when bad things happen, we have to try to learn from those situations. Think about a bad moment in your life, and challenge your thinking around how this event helped you. (Virtue: Optimistic Future-Mindedness)
Week 2	Why does it usually feel good to share our feelings with others? (Skill: Empathy)	Pessimism has been related to stress, anxiety and depression. What could you do today to help combat your negative thoughts and turn them into positive thoughts? (Virtue: Optimistic Future-Mindedness)	If we disagree with someone's perspective, what would be the best thing to do? Have you ever had trouble doing this? (Skill: Social Problem-Solving)	Why might people not listen to new ideas? What helps you to be more likely to listen to new or different ideas? (Skill: Empathy)	Is it helpful to think about our past when paving the way for our future? Why or why not? (Theme: Planning for the Future)
Week 3	Who do you admire most? What are some qualities that you admire about this person? (Theme: Planning for the Future)	Small miracles happen every day. What could you do to raise your awareness of these miracles? (Virtue: Optimistic Future-Mindedness)	What does charity mean to you? Do you need to give money, food, or clothing in order to help others? How else can you do it? (Skill: Social Problem-Solving)	What effects can stress have on the body? Why is important to monitor your stress level? (Virtue: Optimistic Future-Mindedness)	What are you most passionate about? How can you do more of what you love doing? (Theme: Planning for the Future)
Week 4	There are many different ways that help us keep us organized (calendar, apps, planner, etc.). How do you stay organized? (Theme: Planning for the Future)	What is something about your future that you are optimistic about? Why? (Virtue: Optimistic Future-Mindedness)	The person next to you in class keeps trying to look at your paper during a test. What do you do? (Skill: Social Problem-Solving)	What do you like most about being a _____ grader? When do you feel you are at your best in the school? (Virtue: Optimistic Future-Mindedness)	"Don't judge others unless you are standing in their shoes." Do you agree with that quote? What does it have to do with Empathy? (Skill: Empathy)

term *Month Three* to denote the third full month of MCCs, based on beginning in November/Month One; for schools that begin the school year in August, for example, MCCs would start in October/Month Zero and would reference the month numbers, rather than the month names, thereafter.

In Chapter 8, you will find a more comprehensive look at the progression of MCCs for each school year. While this chapter specifically outlines the *Better Me* framework, Chapter 8 shows how students progress from *Better Me* to *Better School* to *Better World* each year that they are provided with MCCs, with the goal of expanding students' worldview and increasing their skills for civic engagement. Although only one full month sample is provided Table 2.2, you can find the entire year of *Better Me* daily prompts in Appendix A, *Better School* in Appendix B, and *Better World* in Appendix C of this book or on the companion website, resources.corwin.com/MorningClassroomConversations.

Figure 2.1 shows how complementary skills and virtues can be integrated into monthly themes. For the sample provided, the complementary skills are empathy and social problem-solving, and the complementary virtue is optimistic future-mindedness. These skills and virtues, along with the overall theme, are cycled throughout each day and week so that there is an equal (or almost equal) amount of conversations for each. Skills and goals are specifically chosen for each month to build upon the overall monthly theme. For example, in order for students to benefit the most from prompts centered on future planning, such as Week 1, Day 2 earlier, they must also have an understanding of how to problem solve in certain situations and have empathy for themselves and those around them. Similarly, optimistic future-mindedness plays a vital role in planning for the future and allows students to set positive goals and have faith in their own abilities.

As you can see, MCCs have an underlying pedagogical structure linked to SECD, along with opportunities to develop conversational skills. Like many good strategies, MCCs can look deceptively simple. For optimal impact, there are a number of guidelines for how to prepare for MCCs and how to organize prompts over the course of a whole year. The next chapter outlines in detail the nuts and bolts of carrying out MCCs and the many different ways prompts can be used.

Chapter Wrap-Up

The MCC approach is multilayered, with each layer equally important to understand and integrate consistently into daily prompts. We reviewed the underlying structure of MCCs and how they prepare students for school and civic engagement through four distinct dimensions (skills, virtues, themes, and developmental progression). We examined how the daily prompts for MCCs provide an opportunity to sharpen students' focus on certain SEL skills, think about and internalize key virtues that promote positive purpose, and discuss themes that are relevant to their life in school. This is all done within a unique, three-year developmental framework, through conversations that allow students to take ownership of the self (*Better Me*), expand to think of themselves as participants in improving their school community (*Better School*), and ultimately see how they can take social action to impact positive change in their neighborhoods and beyond (*Better World*). A sample month is provided as a visual to demonstrate the unique MCC framework in practice.

 Reflective Conversations for Growth

Now that you have reviewed the multiple dimensions and moving parts to MCCs to understand the overall structure, as well as taken a look at one traditional sample month of prompts, reflect on/write down the following and commit to taking the appropriate follow-up actions in order to continue to learn and grow as a Conversation Leader.

ACTION STEPS/PRIORITIES

What skills, virtues, and themes are most needed for your classroom or your school and how can they be used to improve the school? Please choose at least one for each.

_____

_____

_____

ADAPTATIONS

Using thoughts from your Action Steps/Priorities and Figure 2.1 as a starter guide, what will a Year-Long Themes, Virtues, and Skills chart look like in your classroom? How will it be used?

_____

_____

_____

CHALLENGES

What is one challenge you foresee with implementing this framework, taking into consideration the sample month? How can you address this challenge? Who can help?

_____

_____

_____

QUESTIONS

Do you have any questions that remain? Looking to contact the authors? Send an email to MorningClassroomConversations@gmail.com with a specific MCC start to finish question and the authors will get back to you within 48 hours.

_____

_____

_____

CHAPTER 3

Preparation and Introduction of Morning Classroom Conversations

Getting familiar with the process of Morning Classroom Conversations (MCCs) and prepping to implement this program with your students may seem like a big task, which is why this chapter is here to assist! There are some important first steps that you can take as a Conversation Leader to help you and your students in preparing for and starting MCCs. Doing so will allow for a smooth and efficient transition into group discussion. This chapter addresses all the factors necessary to consider before beginning your MCCs, such as selecting the appropriate number and order of prompts, establishing conversation norms with your students, and setting up a safe and secure environment for students to feel comfortable and ready to listen, share, and engage.

 ## SELECTING MCC PROMPTS

The essence of MCCs is a conversation-starting statement referred to as a "prompt." In order to provide Conversation Leaders with easy-to-follow access to a comprehensive list of prompts, a full collection of these prompts are provided for three sequential school years. As outlined in the sample Year-Long Themes, Virtues, and Skills chart provided in Chapter 2 (Figure 2.1), these prompts comprise what is called the "MCC Full Sequence." In other words, the Full Sequence of prompts encompasses *all* the virtues, skills, themes, and developmental progression that was discussed in Chapter 2.

Given the realities of school schedules, it is possible that circumstances will not allow for implementing MCCs by following the MCC Full Sequence (November/Month One to June/Month Eight) provided in Appendices A, B, and C. Even when Conversation Leaders are provided the daily allotment of 10 to 15 minutes per prompt, you will find that everything does not "go as planned" in a school day, week, or month. Snow days, professional development days, instructional rounds and other school visitations, standardized testing schedules, and other disruptions will mean that every possible day to do an MCC will not contain an MCC. This will require some modifications in how prompts are selected. There are other considerations that may influence the tailoring of prompts in your classroom and school context. Do not let these unpredictabilities deter your success in having productive MCCs; here's how you can practice flexibility!

NEEDS ASSESSMENT

The need for building students' conversation skills has been described as virtually universal. However, any new program coming into school will be strongest if it matches your population and situation. The *way* in which MCCs will improve your classroom is certainly something worth exploring before beginning your MCC journey. For example, at-risk and diverse youth benefit from MCCs by using these conversations as a way to give themselves a voice, to make their varying needs heard, and to provide them with the tools to become autonomous in their own life. Similarly, classrooms that struggle with teacher and student relationships or find there is a need to improve the overall feeling of community can benefit from MCCs by using it to build trust within the classroom and give students an active role in making their classroom better. Of course, MCCs can also be used as a preventive measure to further improve upon the strengths that your classroom has or prevent various classroom climate issues from occurring or worsening.

It is equally important to look at what areas may require more support for social, emotional, and behavioral growth. As you as a school professional know, there are developmental issues common across contexts, such as the difficulty students often experience when transitioning into sixth grade or ninth grade or are otherwise starting the school year in a new environment, in addition to the myriad of physical and emotional changes that occur among middle school-aged students as they grow and develop. However, community composition, socioeconomic status, adverse childhood events (ACEs), proportion of special education students, and several other factors can also directly impact the classroom and school environment and thus must be acknowledged. The reality in schools today is that many more students are likely to be experiencing ACEs than educators are aware of. Hence, all social-emotional learning (SEL)–related interventions should be trauma-informed, that is, sensitive to students' strong emotional experiences (Pawlo et al., 2019).

Even though MCCs have been created to be trauma-informed, specific needs such as community violence, bullying in school or on social media, theft within or outside of the school, and drug use should be kept in mind when implementing MCCs. Based on these considerations, you can review the prompts that have been developed and make modifications and/or create your own prompts to be most in line with what would fit best for your students' needs. To help investigate this directly, it always is helpful to poll students to gain better insight into what they perceive their needs to be. Have they witnessed or become a victim of frequent bullying? Have they witnessed or become a victim of theft? Have they witnessed or taken part in drug use? Are they concerned about other school safety factors? Are they concerned with relationships between students and staff or general school connectedness? These are just a few crucial questions that can be asked, and initially, they are best answered anonymously through a survey to ensure reliability of the answers given. If further inquiry leads to a discovery of a specific area to target in MCCs, then this factor should be fully integrated into the preestablished daily prompt and monthly themes. You may tailor MCC prompts by doing the following.

ADJUSTING THE NUMBER OF MCCS TO MATCH SCHOOL CALENDARS

When using the MCC Full Sequence document (Appendices A–C) for your daily MCC structure, there may be instances where you have more prompts than necessary in a given week, since the MCC Full Sequence document was created to follow a standard five days per week schedule, and school calendars frequently can deviate from this. You can address these situations with slight adjustments. To prepare for this possibility, it is recommended that Conversation Leaders view the upcoming week's prompts in advance to ensure that there is a preselected prompt assigned for each school day based on your discretion and preference. You likely will find that you have extra prompts that you can "collect" and use for the times when you need additional, or alternative, prompts.

In planning your MCCs, your school calendar will serve as a guide for the expected amount of prompts needed. If you notice an upcoming day off that will remove one of the five potential school days, then it will be at your discretion to choose which prompts are discussed that week. One strategy for doing this is to review your MCC virtues, skills, and themes page. What is the theme for that month? What is the virtue? What skills are addressed? Then, you can review what might have priority for that shorter week and select prompts accordingly. For example, if Conversation Leaders are approaching a November holiday break for Thanksgiving, they will likely need to decide upon three of the five provided prompts for that week and may choose to keep the skill-focused prompts versus the theme- or virtue-focused prompts. The Conversation Leader may determine that the students need more support in skill building, especially if they were not incorporated as much in previous weeks.

The MCC Full Sequence uses a four-week structure, with some months requiring a fifth week of instruction. These months would require supplemental prompts that can be created based on your classroom-specific needs. For example, if the month of March starts on a Monday and your school does not have any days off that month, there will be three additional days in March during the fifth week that will need additional prompts. One strategy for creating these prompts is to reference your version of Figure 2.1 from Chapter 2 and decide what is best to focus on (e.g., theme, virtue, skill, or all three). You can also reference other prompts discussed that month. Was there any prompt that worked particularly well for your class that may warrant readdressing or expanding on? Was there a topic mentioned that allowed for similar or more specific prompts to follow up? Additionally, there always will be the option of creating your own prompt that follows that month's structure, if you are inspired to do so!

SORTING AND REORDERING OF MCCS

Although the Full Sequence of prompts was made with a specific structure in mind, this MCC sequence is only confined to monthly structural outlines and has a great deal of flexibility from day to day or even week to week. Using your Year-Long Themes, Virtues, and Skills chart as a guide, you may review prompts that are outlined for a given month and decide ahead of time (or the morning of!) that certain prompts would be better incorporated if placed on a different day or week. Perhaps a certain prompt is better in line with other programs and strategies implemented in your school or classroom, works well with an academic topic that will be introduced that day, or relates to current events.

For example, for the month of April/Month Six, where prompts center around leadership and connecting to others, a Conversation Leader who teaches social studies may look at the daily prompts and how they can best match with the curriculum that month, such as discussions on presidents, advocates for social justice, or otherwise influential people in the world in the past and present day. As long as the prompts are delivered consistently and follow a monthly structure similar or identical to the Year-Long Themes, Virtues, and Skills chart provided in Chapter 2 (Figure 2.1), the ordering options can suit particular needs and schedules!

INCORPORATING TOPICAL INFORMATION

Another important flexibility that MCCs provide is the ability to add in prompts that are in line with topical current events as they occur. All Conversation Leaders should be prepared for possible events happening in your local or larger community that are crucial to address as they occur. These events could be anything from local tragedies to political events, events related to the economy, or events impacting race/gender/ethnicity. Events like the COVID-19 pandemic cannot be anticipated in a curriculum but must be addressed. This applies to any event that brings about social unrest and protest. There may be instances where a current event comes up that morning and the prompt for that day will need to be altered or switched to be in line with the event. Alternatively, there could be a planned event coming up, such as elections or court rulings, where you might want to anticipate and have a conversation starter ready in advance.

To help envision situations that would require prompts geared toward topical events and how to choose these prompts, here are two different examples of both a planned and unplanned current event.

Example 1: Mrs. Sanchez is reviewing the November/Month One prompts for her seventh-grade class and realized she would like to incorporate more discussion about local, state, and federal elections into her prompts that month. She plans to spend some time in her academic classes reviewing the election process but feels it is important to discuss the character development aspect of the elected officials and the impact that voting can make on communities. Taking into consideration the theme, virtue, and skills addressed in November, Mrs. Sanchez saw several natural connections with the preestablished prompts for that month regarding the virtue (Constructive Creativity) and the theme (a focus on Making the World Better). She was easily able to select prompts throughout the months and alter them to focus more on the impact of the election process or by simply adding variations of "How can this apply to the election process and its impact on society?"

Example 2: Mr. Ross has been consistently using MCCs each morning for his sixth-grade class and is in the middle of the March/Month Five prompts when he discovers one evening that there has been a shooting in his school community that led to several people becoming critically injured. He knew that his students would be aware of the event and would be discussing it with each other. Mr. Ross felt that MCCs were an ideal opportunity to discuss how his students feel regarding this tragic event and checking to see if they feel safe in his classroom. Since February/Month Four focused on the theme of Showing Resilience and Overcoming Obstacles, Mr. Ross thought it necessary to revisit a prompt from the previous month and look at it from the lens of those affected by the recent event. This helped his students recall and strengthen their lessons from the February/Month Four prompts as well as helped them discuss the event and work through their emotions and how this may impact how they feel at school.

Both of the preceding examples require creative brainstorming and deep consideration into how your Year-Long Themes, Virtues, and Skills chart can assist you in aligning the events with the MCC framework to continue building crucial SEL skills, but also helping students remain aware and knowledgeable about events happening in their community. MCCs are meant to allow a space for students to process their surrounding environment through conversation, as adolescents need this in order to feel connected. By talking about current events, they are better able to focus on academic content afterward. In order to be most effective, MCCs, and SEL in general, must be flexibly adapted to their environments to best suit the changing needs of students.

 ## ESTABLISHING MCC NORMS AND A PRODUCTIVE CLASSROOM CLIMATE

A major step in building a foundation of success with MCCs is fostering the appropriate climate. Educators understand that a classroom or group cannot function effectively without caring student–teacher relationships and a supportive climate of trust. Indeed, what we know about learning and the brain implies that caring relationships are essential for lasting learning. There have been ample studies in these areas to help support the notion that academic success can be both directly and indirectly affected by their relationships with their teachers. This is in part because those students who perceive their relationship with their teacher to be a positive and caring one will have the benefit of having a supportive environment in which to actively and appropriately engage with their academics (McClain, 2019). Similarly, students with perceived negative relationships with their teachers are at a higher risk for struggling academically. Namely, critique and feedback from teachers to their students that are centered on personal attributes of the student have shown negative impact on students rating of their relationship with their teacher (Skipper & Douglas, 2015), which can ultimately affect other factors such as the child's academic achievement.

The above points lead to an overall impression that an environment of trust supports academic growth and encourages positive behavior, which will make the MCCs (as well as other classes) most effective. Although this type of climate is undoubtedly beneficial for all areas of a student's school environment, the MCCs especially require all participants to feel comfortable and supported in order to allow for true social and emotional growth. When students do not feel trust, support, and respect, they will feel hesitant to share their true thoughts and feelings and in turn will not be open to hearing the thoughts and feelings of others. Under those circumstances, genuine exchange is unlikely.

The feelings of trust, safety, and comfort that teachers want for their students do not happen automatically. Explicit efforts must be made to help students feel safe and understood prior to carrying out MCCs, and these efforts must be revisited over time to ensure all students feel that they have a brave space for participating in MCCs. The brave space concept (discussed in detail shortly) is introduced as a realistic alternative to safe space, which all too often is declared by adults but not experienced by students. This seemingly small nuance creates a more supportive and participatory environment. *Brave spaces* for MCCs can be created in several ways, such as creating classroom norms, gradually guiding students into expected MCC routines, and using your skills as a Conversation Leader to guide successful discussions. This section hones in on these strategies and what they might look like in your classroom or group setting.

THE BRAVE SPACE CONCEPT

As an educator, you have likely heard of the term "safe space." While the origin of the term is unclear, it has undoubtedly incited some controversy and deep misunderstanding. A safe space is put forward as, and understood as, a place where students can speak their truth, share their feelings and opinions, and be assured of no negative judgment and no reprisal. While this space can be "declared," the conditions of safety implied cannot. Either through intuition or direct or learned experience, students come to realize that the promised safety typically does not occur. Revelations in the safe space get shared, often on social media; negative reactions, subtle and substantial, take place in the space itself; and verbal and nonverbal behaviors reveal judgments being made—something about which adolescents are especially sensitive. Adults may declare a safe space, but too often, that is not the case.

In many ways, brave spaces can be thought of as a particular kind of safe space, one that must be created and consistently nurtured within a classroom environment in order to allow for productive and meaningful conversations between students and educators. The main components of a brave space include the following:

- "Controversy with civility," where varying opinions are accepted
- "Owning intentions and impacts," in which students acknowledge and discuss instances where a dialogue has affected the emotional well-being of another person

- "Challenge by choice," where students have an option to step in and out of challenging conversations

- "Respect," where students show respect for one another's basic personhood

- "No attacks," where students agree not to intentionally inflict harm on one another (Ali, 2007)

Perhaps most vital, no one makes a guarantee of safety. Therefore, participation in the space is defined as "brave." It risks negative consequences. Brave spaces, and the main components within them, are not formed overnight, but they are certainly worth the effort! Do not be intimidated by this, as forming brave spaces within a classroom is possible but requires commitment and consistency.

There are a few explicit ways that brave spaces can be created in your classroom. The most fundamental is to lead by example. Your showing the level of respect, vulnerability, and accountability that you would like to see in your students is necessary if any other measures are to succeed. And those measures involve concerted efforts to provide your students with a physical and mental space where students feel comfortable and assured that they will be given the ample opportunity to share their feelings and experiences (Morton, 2020).

This brings up another motivation behind creating brave spaces: to offer an environment where marginalized groups can speak freely and leave the classroom feeling heard, respected, and understood. A brave space, within the context of MCCs, is an environment which fosters social justice by allowing "full and equitable participation of people from all social identity groups in a [classroom] that is mutually shaped to meet their needs" (Adams et al., 2016, p. 3). Once the brave space is established in your classroom, you are likely to see a noticeable change in openness and participation from students, within both MCCs and academic content areas. Setting up classroom norms specific to MCCs, with students playing an active role in this process, is discussed further next.

MCC NORMS

Those facilitating MCCs will need to set the stage for civil and effective classroom discussions. As educators, you are aware that this will require clearly communicated rules or norms that the students must follow. For this reason, the first week in the introductory month of October/Month Zero allows for time dedicated to creating the norms. MCC norms may be similar to general classroom norms in many ways but ideally will be tailored to group discussions. This is the time to introduce the brave space concept mentioned earlier and what that means for your students, to set a strong foundation for the direction that your classroom as a whole will want to go regarding classroom expectations. After discussing the classroom goal of creating a brave space, the best way to create MCCs norms is to collaborate with the students in your class to establish these norms so that everyone is aware of what is expected and so students feel responsible for following the guidelines that they helped to establish. Students may very well have input on MCCs norms that teachers have not thought of!

Involving students in creating MCC norms relies on the brainstorming process. There are certain open-ended questions that can be asked of your students to help them think of how to avoid common problematic issues that arise during large group discussions. Questions such as "How will we prevent talking over others?" "How will we let others know when we want to talk?" and "What if we disagree with someone?" will allow students to brainstorm the best way to have a respectful and efficient MCC. This process can also include students writing out what kinds of classroom environments work best for them, moving into small groups to share these ideas with their classmates, then having those groups of students share out their most consistent ideas, either in person in the classroom or in an electronic format. You can then take these ideas and create a universal list that works best for everyone.

Conversation Leaders and students must also collaborate on procedures for nonverbal communication, body language, voice volume, speaking time, and appropriate language and topics, among others. Some examples of this include making eye contact, facing the speaker or audience, speaking clearly and concisely, and keeping the topic applicable and appropriate, in addition to any other strategies that you feel your students may need extra practice or support with.

You have an active role in creating an environment of inclusion and making sure everyone gets equal opportunity to share their thoughts. In order to ensure this, you must always be cognizant of any intrinsic bias with regard to calling on students or prompting students to share and participate. Everyone has, at one point or another, shown bias in how they act toward others, but being aware of this and making a concerted effort to avoid it will make a world of difference for your students. It may be beneficial to explore these biases prior to MCCs. Ask yourself if you have had any personal experiences that may impact your thoughts, feelings, or opinions toward certain students, certain circumstances, or even specific prompts. These biases are not anything to disregard or be ashamed of. Indeed, the only way to successfully reverse the effects of these biases is to fully embrace and be aware of them. If you, for example, find that you may have subtle preferences with choosing students of a certain personality, gender, race, ethnicity, ability level, or otherwise, be sure to provide equal opportunity for those who are not called on or included as often.

If you feel unsure of your potential implicit preferences, consider keeping a log of students whom you've called on for a week or more, in order to give you a clearer image of your preferences and how to work against them to create more equality and balanced participation in your classroom. All of this contributes to "walking the walk" of creating a supportive, trusting environment for all students and increasing overall participation.

With your norms established and awareness of your biases, it may be beneficial to revisit the brave space as an explicit concept so that your students can start to make connections with how MCC norms will help foster this type of environment. Discuss with students why they feel these norms are in place. Are they there to restrict students' voice and autonomy? Are they there to get students in trouble? Of course not! In fact, the opposite is true. You may know this, but not all students will have a clear idea of *why* these norms are needed and how beneficial they actually are with regard to creating a brave space.

If time allows after establishing your MCC norms, it may even help to have students role-play situations where the norms are not followed (within reason), and when they are, so that students can get an idea of how much better their classroom climate will feel when these norms are in place. Think of these norms and expectations as guard rails, keeping your class on the path to success with MCCs. Occasionally revisiting these norms ensues that the rails are correctly placed to maintain the journey. Establishing these norms and rules prior to introducing MCCs, and revisiting as needed, protects the supportive climate and allows for students to form genuine exchange.

There are many components of being a successful Conversation Leader, though certain strategies and responsibilities of Conversation Leaders directly relate to fostering a productive classroom climate. A Conversation Leader must build the feeling of a caring and secure environment for students and constantly maintain that feeling by being an active participant and effective moderator of each MCC. As mentioned earlier, one way to do this is to revisit the MCC norms frequently, potentially keeping them visible in the classroom during conversations and adapt as appropriate. It is difficult to comprise a full list of norms and guidelines for an activity that students, and perhaps even yourself, are new to, which is why it is important to consider the MCC norms as a working list that must be constantly reviewed.

Chapter Wrap-Up

Selecting the prompts for MCC conversations is an essential activity. We highlighted some effective models for doing so as well as provided samples that have been used successfully. MCCs work best when Conversation Leaders create caring relationships and a supportive climate of trust, which allow for more engagement and participation. We showed how to use the concept of "brave space" as a foundation for this climate, working in collaboration with students to establish MCC norms and expectations that are revisited periodically throughout the year.

Reflective Conversations for Growth

Now that you have familiarized yourself with strategies in selecting, reducing, or altering prompts and creating classroom MCC norms, reflect on/ write down the following and commit to taking the appropriate follow-up actions in order to continue to learn and grow as a Conversation Leader.

ACTION STEPS/PRIORITIES

Which of the discussed prompt selection strategies will be most helpful for your classroom/teaching context?

_____

_____

_____

(Continued)

What will MCC norms look like in your classroom? What norms will be most important to you students for successful MCCs? How can you be sure to integrate MCC norms with other norms you have established?

_____

_____

_____

CHALLENGES

If a prompt has less traction in your group than others, how do you plan to keep your students engaged for the minimum 10 minutes, rather than cutting the conversation short or skipping it altogether?

_____

_____

_____

QUESTIONS

What questions still remain after reading Chapter 3? Consider submitting 1 to 2 questions to the authors at MorningClassroomConversations@gmail.com.

_____

_____

_____

CHAPTER 4

Setting the Foundation for Morning Classroom Conversations Through Practice

B efore the curtain opens for a play, a crew will effectively place props, stage scenery, and arrange lighting to create the desired "scene." In the same way, when teachers also "set the stage" for Morning Classroom Conversations (MCCs) before they actually start, everything is likely to go more smoothly. So, rather than immediately jumping into in-depth conversations, it is suggested to use the first month to prepare for the official start of MCCs (i.e., *a preparatory period*). In an effort to demonstrate the pre-MCC nature, this preparatory period is called "October/Month Zero." (This reflects that some schools open in August and others in September; if your school opens in August, September would be your "Month Zero" and your preparatory period; for most schools in the United States, September is the start and October would be the preparatory "Month Zero.") If your school year runs from September to June and you are a Conversation Leader using a daily home-room structure, it is suggested that you use the month of September to learn about your new class. "Month Zero" is used subsequently to set the foundation and create expectations about MCCs. Beginning with simple conversation starters (provided later) allows students an opportunity to become comfortable with the structure of discussing topics as a class, to practice applying their established MCC norms, and to form a solid foundation for a brave space, as discussed in Chapter 3.

From early childhood, many children are reminded that practice allows for skill building and effective preparation. The same goes for MCCs! By "practicing," teachers and students are able to learn about timing and logistics. For instance, a Conversation Leader may find that it's the same few students always responding as you introduce MCCs. If this happens, it may cause other students to check out of the conversations. By recognizing this issue early in a preparatory period, a Conversation Leader can problem solve around ways of expanding participation. On the other hand, it is also possible that conversation wrap-up becomes challenging. If Conversation Leaders recognize this, they can read more about conversation wrap-up strategies and be better prepared for keeping conversations within the allotted 10- to 15-minute time frame for when MCCs begin in November/Month One.

The preparatory period focuses on factors related to the environment, routine, and pacing that may be important to explore. For instance, the physical arrangement may look different depending on your room and the size of the group. By using October/Month Zero for preparation, the layout of the room can be established prior rather than coordinating where students are sitting and delaying true MCC topics. Establishing clear patterns and routines will be imperative for MCC effectiveness. If both Conversation Leaders and students know the expectations, there will be less confusion. Pacing is another factor to consider, which may vary depending on personalities within the group. How long should the prompt be presented? How long should students be able to comment? Should students be able to directly comment on other students' replies? All these answers can be explored by practicing as a group.

ADAPTATIONS TO REMOTE PLATFORMS

Depending on your circumstance, there may be a need to have conversations remotely. MCCs, as well as the preparation period of October, are designed to fit well into online platforms such as Zoom and Google Classroom, though the logistics mentioned earlier may look slightly different. For example, in order to create a structured environment all students may spend the MCC muted unless they are speaking, students may need to sign on 2 minutes before the MCC starts to ensure that the teacher has enough time to allow everyone into the classroom, or there may be more likelihood for students to speak over each other without the ability to recognize social cues. If lessons are being held remotely, the structure of introducing MCCs during a *preparatory period* allows teachers to teach "Zoom etiquette," explore technological issues and note different options such as grid/gallery mode, how to do pair-shares in breakout rooms, and procedures for volunteering to speak or comment on others' responses.

SAMPLE SCRIPTS FOR OCTOBER/MONTH ZERO FOR YEARS 1–3

The structure of the sample provided uses a four-week period: Week 1 as an introduction, Week 2 as an opportunity to "break the ice," and Weeks 3 and 4 to introduce the skills, virtues, and themes of MCCs. Weeks 1 and 2 have the most flexibility, so students get a chance to become used to the structure of conversations and learn how the norms will provide a safe climate for responding and for disagreement. Weeks 3 and 4 cover foundational concepts—virtues and skills—within the preparation period so that students are able to dive into topics at a deeper level once the MCCs begin in November/Month One.

Additionally, you will note that each week is labeled 1 through 5, to represent five weekdays, Monday through Friday. Depending on the calendar year, this may not fit exactly with each schools' schedule, therefore minor adjustments may be necessary, such as those discussed in Chapter 3. Another important topic mentioned in Chapter 3 that ties heavily to the preparation period is creating a brave space. Efforts must be made to help students feel safe and understood prior to carrying out MCCs, and these efforts must be revisited over time to ensure all students feel that they have a brave space for participating in MCCs. The October/Month Zero preparation period is the perfect time to establish this! Additionally, strategic introduction to MCCs can increase students' commitment to these activities. As they understand the value of MCCs for themselves, their participation will grow in frequency and depth.

To help everyone grasp MCCs more easily, a developmental structure is recommended. Week 1 presents basic concepts, sets the stage for how MCCs will be conducted, and begins with some simple practice activities:

Day 1: Introduction to MCCs

Day 2: Setting norms and expectations for the group

Day 3: Practice of understanding norms

Days 4 and 5: Icebreakers

Week 2 continues with icebreakers for practice. Feel free to either use or exchange the activity suggestions; don't hesitate to use your favorite icebreaker activities instead!

As mentioned, the goal of Weeks 3 and 4 is to introduce students to the MCC framework (which was presented comprehensively in Chapter 2) in a developmentally appropriate way. Activities during those weeks give students a unique opportunity to explore virtues, skills, and themes that will guide all future conversations. Without this preparatory period, students may lack common language (e.g., Positive Purpose) or be unclear on the meaning of terms like Emotion Regulation. These suggested prompts serve as an introduction for Year 1 and potentially a review for Years 2 and 3.

As with any program, students in Years 2 and 3 may have a different degree of understanding. Maybe students have joined your class or group who have moved into the area and have never heard of an MCC before. It is possible that past teachers' buy-in to a program differed, leaving some students with more familiarity and comfort with MCC structures than others. The month of preparation is a unique opportunity to "even the playing field" and ensure that students are starting the first true month of MCCs (i.e., November/Month One) with a similar level of understanding. You will see language in Years 2 and 3 that recognizes the MCCs may be new, or relatively new, to some students with whom you are working.

The rest of this chapter provides sample scripts for the *preparatory period* (i.e., the month of October/Month Zero if using the suggested MCC structure) that you should, of course, adapt for your style and comfort.

1. This school year, our class will be taking about 15 minutes each morning to discuss a variety of topics. Some of these topics will be easy to answer and others will make you think deeply. These discussions are going to help us explore our own thoughts and feelings, get to know our class, practice our skills for discussion and respectful debate, as well as several other skills that are crucial for purposeful living. We will talk more about these skills later this month, but this week we will start by going over classroom norms for our discussions and engaging in some get-to-know-you questions to warm us up for our Morning Classroom Conversation topics for this school year. Let's discuss some questions I have for you about our MCCs and feel free to ask any of your own questions as well!

   a. Why do you think having regular classroom discussions in ___ grade is important?

   b. How do conversations help you live a purposeful life at school?

   c. What might be some challenges we will face as a class with these discussions? How can we address these challenges together?

   d. What kinds of questions are you anticipating?

2. Yesterday, we discussed a little bit about what our morning will be like with the Morning Classroom Conversations. This month, we will be starting off by going over classroom norms and practicing our conversations within the classroom with some get-to-know you questions. Today, we will start by discussing some rules and expectations for these discussions (the norms below are suggestions that can be adjusted to fit your classroom, added to your existing norms, etc.):

   a. Wait to share your thoughts or answers until it is your turn to speak.

   b. Respect others turn to talk by listening quietly and keeping your answers to a reasonable length.

   c. Be accepting to others' thoughts and ideas—you may share your disagreements thoughtfully and respectfully, when appropriate and/or if time permits.

   d. Use respectful and school-appropriate language.

   e. If you have something to share and did not get to, you may share it with me after class, write it down for our MCC box or submit an MCC Google form.

3. Having "norms" lets everyone know what is expected/unexpected during MCCs, and how we can proceed in a way that allows everyone to be heard. In order to practice, today we are going to play a game of this or that. I want you to put your thumb up/down based on the option that you prefer and after we all signal for that item, we can take turns telling why we picked what we did. We will have a chance to share after each item.

- (put your thumb up if you prefer …) Winter or (your thumb down if you prefer …) summer
- Beach or mountains
- iPhone or Android

4. One thing you don't know about me is …

5. What is the easiest way for someone else to make you smile?

WEEK 2

1. This week we are going to practice a few more conversation starters. We will try to do one every day, as a practice for the structure of our MCC. Today, we are going to do another round of this or that. I want you to put your thumb up if you prefer … and thumb down if you prefer …
   a. Dogs or cats
   b. Sunrise or sunset
   c. Ice cream or cookies

2. Have you ever accidentally fallen asleep in a public place? Where and why?

3. If you could give $100 to charity, which one would you choose? Why?

4. What do you think is the best way to show people that you care about them?

5. If you could start a restaurant based around one main ingredient, one meal (breakfast, lunch, and dinner) or one food group, what would it be? Why?

WEEK 3

1. Now that we have had a chance to practice with some informal conversation starters, the next couple of weeks will introduce you to some of the skills and virtues that our MCCs will target. We will discuss a different one each day. You will have an opportunity to learn about these areas and consider how they support the development of a "Better you." This week, we will review important virtues that make us better people. Virtues are part of our character. We will focus on these:

   (1) **Optimistic Future-Mindedness;**
   (2) **Compassionate Forgiveness and Gratitude;**
   (3) **Responsible Diligence;**
   (4) **Helpful Generosity;** and
   (5) **Constructive Creativity**

   For instance, let's talk about

   Optimistic Future-Mindedness thumbs up or thumbs down—or just hold up your fist if you are not sure—for this statement: It's better to see the glass as half empty than half full. Why? [Be sure to communicate the fact that people who see the glass as half full are usually happier and more successful.] That's why **Optimistic Future-Mindedness**—and all the virtues we will discuss—are virtues. They are good things to have as part of your character. Maybe not for every single thing and situation but definitely most of the time.

2. Today, we are going to talk about **Compassionate Forgiveness and Gratitude**. Think of a time that you forgave someone using compassion. What do you think is the difference between forgiving someone with compassion and without compassion? Are you grateful that the forgiveness happened? Why or why not? Reflecting on your past can be a very helpful way to choose gratitude and to be forgiving. Take a moment to think about people you are grateful for.

3. **Responsible Diligence** means using careful and persistent effort to take on your duty within a situation. Being a responsible person will support your development into the best version of yourself. Why do you think this is true? What responsibilities do you take on now that you hope to keep doing throughout your life? How is responsible diligence like a promise you make to yourself?

4. Let's talk about **Helpful Generosity**. At times, individuals are more focused on their "selfies" than others. What does generosity mean to you? What do you do to help others? Think about small things, everyday things, in particular. How do these actions make you feel? [Be sure to discuss that when people give willingly and perform charitable acts, our bodies release several "happiness chemicals" including oxytocin to our brains. In other words, we feel good when we are able to see others feel good.]

5. Our last virtue for this week is **Constructive Creativity**, which means using your imagination in a purposeful way. When you hear the word creativity, your immediate thought might go to creativity within artistic work. Are there other ways to be creative? For instance, how might creativity impact your ability to form/sustain friendships? Who are people that you consider to be **constructively creative**? What is it about them that makes you give them that label?

Wrap-up of Week 3: Great job with our first set of MCC key concepts this week. Next week, we will review the skills we need to act on the virtues and positive purpose.

WEEK 4

1. Last week, we took some time to discuss a few different virtues that can help better ourselves. Who wants to remind the class in their own words what a virtue is? Who remembers the virtues we covered? This week, we will be discussing skills that will help us act on these virtues. These skills are **Communication, Empathy, Emotional Regulation,** and **Social Problem-Solving**. We will also be discussing another virtue that can apply to everything we do, **Positive Purpose**. **Positive Purpose** incorporates all of our other virtues, as well as all of the skills we will be discussing this week. It is so important for adolescents to develop a sense of purpose, or a deeper meaning of how each of you can make the world—your community, your family, your school, and yourself—better and to be able to communicate that clearly to others. That's the reason you want to act with virtues and use your skills. One way to do that is to think about yourself and how you want to be a better communicator of your purpose. Imagine at the end of the school year, the principal will call you up to the front of the auditorium, with all the other students there, and tell everyone what **Positive Purpose** for yourself that you have accomplished. What would you want the principal to say? If we address areas in which we hope to improve, we are more likely to develop a better version of ourselves. What is an area

that you are working on to become the best version of yourself? What is the first step you can take to making these improvements?

2. Today, we have a discussion topic that builds on communication, which we talked about yesterday: **Empathy.** Who can define **empathy** for me in their own words (empathy is the understanding and sharing of another's feelings, often accompanied by a desire to help them)? How is **empathy** different from sympathy? How can **empathy** improve how we communicate?

3. Another skill that is important to be able to act on our virtues is **Emotional Regulation**. This refers to the ability to be aware of and handle our strong emotions so that they don't take over our actions. We all experience a wide range of emotions, sometimes feeling several at one time. Give an example of a time you felt a powerful emotion and you were able to maintain control over it. How did you do it? Did you find a better way to express those feelings? [Be sure to label these as examples of different ways to regulate emotions—like breathing, counting, leaving the situation, distracting oneself, etc.]

4. Today, we will be discussing our final skill, **Social Problem-Solving**. Social situations can be complicated at times. It's helpful to have a strategy for thinking it through and trying to solve it. What are some common problems you experience in social situations with friends and family? What are some strategies that you and/or your family/friends have used to solve a social problem? Were there other skills used for these strategies (communication, empathy, and emotional regulation)? If so, which ones?

5. Everyone did a great job contributing to some very positive conversations this month while reviewing a lot of important terms in the process! Throughout the rest of the school year, there will be a range of skills and virtues that we will work on during our MCCs. Additionally, we will have a monthly theme to help us maintain some consistency within our conversations (feel free to show a visual like Figure 2.1 in Chapter 2, if you find it helpful).

October/Month Zero Year 2

1. Some of you likely had the opportunity to engage in Morning Classroom Conversations last year. Raise your hand if you remember having MCCs! If you did not have MCCs last year, there is no need to worry. We will all be exploring Year 2 together! Let's first review what Morning Classroom Conversations are.

   This school year, our class will be taking some time each morning to discuss a variety of topics. Some of these topics will be easy to answer, and others will make you think deeply. These discussions are going to help us explore our own thoughts and feelings, get to know our class, practice our skills for discussion and respectful debate, as well as several other skills that are crucial for purposeful living. We will talk more about these skills later this month, but this week we will start by going over classroom norms for our discussions, and engaging in some get-to-know-you questions to warm us up for our Morning Classroom Conversation topics for this school year. Let's discuss some questions I have for you about our MCCs and feel free to ask any of your own questions as well!

   a. Why do you think having regular classroom discussions in ___ grade is important?

   b. How do conversations help you live a purposeful life at school?

   c. What might be some challenges we will face as a class with these discussions? How can we address these challenges together?

   d. What kinds of questions are you anticipating?

2. Now that we discussed what our morning will be like with the Morning Classroom Conversations, we must also discuss some rules and expectations for these discussions (the norms that follow are suggestions that can be adjusted to fit your classroom and can be generated with your class).

   a. Wait to share your thoughts or answers until it is your turn to speak.

   b. Respect others turn to talk by listening quietly and keeping your answers to a reasonable length.

   c. Be accepting to others' thoughts and ideas—you may share your disagreements thoughtfully and respectfully, when appropriate and/or if time permits.

   d. Use respectful and school-appropriate language.

   e. If you have something to share and did not get to, you may share it with me after class, write it down for our MCC box or submit an MCC Google form.

3. Heads down thumbs up for the following questions (you can put your heads up after each question and we will have a brief discussion):

   a. [Put your thumb up if you] … have ever had breakfast for dinner?

   b. … if you have ever read a book cover to cover in one day?

   c. … if you enjoy playing video games?

4. What is something that you think people your age understand but adults do not?

5. If you just met someone and had only one question you were able to ask to determine if you would be friends with them, what would that question be? What answer would you like them to have? Why?

1. This week we are going to practice a few more conversation starters. We will try to do one every day, as a practice for the structure of our MCC. Heads down thumbs up for the following questions (heads up after each question with optional brief discussion)
   a. Do you know how to explain what your parent or parents do for a living if someone asked?
   b. Would you go into outer space if given the chance?
   c. If someone wanted to make a movie of your life for all to see, would you let them?

2. If you could create your own subject in school to be most helpful for your future, what would it be?

3. Would you prefer to work on a project together in a group or alone? Why?

4. What is your favorite time period in history? What do you think your life would be like if you lived in that time period?

5. What was your favorite game to play when you were younger?

1. Now that we have had a chance to practice with some informal conversation starters, our next couple weeks will review some of the skills and virtues that you learned about in your first year of MCCs. We will discuss a different one each day. Last year, we targeted *Better Me*, or how these areas can help you become a better version of yourself. This year, we will expand by thinking about how these skills and virtues can help develop a better school. Our goal this week is to review important virtues that make our school a better place for everyone. Virtues are part of our character. We will focus on these:

   (1) **Optimistic Future-Mindedness;**
   (2) **Compassionate Forgiveness and Gratitude;**
   (3) **Responsible Diligence;**
   (4) **Helpful Generosity;** and
   (5) **Constructive Creativity**

   Who can recall these virtues from last year? Does anyone remember what they mean?

   Let's start by talking about Optimistic Future-Mindedness thumbs up–thumbs down—or just hold up your fist if you are not sure—for this statement: Using an optimistic eye toward your future can make it feel more positive and impactful. How do you think your attitude (either optimistic or pessimistic) could impact your success at school? [Discuss the importance of believing in yourself and how that can impact a student's success.]

2. Today, we are going to talk about **Compassionate Forgiveness and Gratitude.** What are some aspects of school for which you are grateful? What are some things about school that you don't like? How would it help you to have **Compassionate Forgiveness** for some of these situations? [Be sure to review the importance of forgiveness toward your own well-being and how compassion allows you to dig deeper into the reasons why one may have engaged in the behavior for which you were holding resentment toward them. Discuss the importance of **Gratitude** in showing appreciation and readiness to return kindness.]

3. **Responsible Diligence** has two parts: responsibility and diligence. What do each of these mean? Why are they connected? What is your responsibility as a student within this school? What types of tasks are you currently responsible for? Are you more or less likely to meet your responsibilities in school if you are diligent about them? Think of some areas that you believe the school can improve. Are there any other areas where you can utilize more diligence to take ownership over making this school a better place?

4. Today, we are going to be talking about **Helpful Generosity**. What would happen to our school if we did not help each other? How does generosity make our school a better place? [Be sure to target the idea that giving promotes cooperation and social connection, which are both very important for strengthening a positive community within your school.]

5. Our last virtue for this week is **Constructive Creativity,** which means using your imagination in a positive, purposeful way. Making schools the best place they can be requires novel ideas and comfort in trying out new ways. How can our school encourage students to share creative ideas to help our school become a better place? Think beyond artistic ability, and about what other types of creativity there are.

Wrap-up of Week 3: Great job with our first set of MCC key virtues this week. Next week, we will introduce the skills we need to act on the virtues and positive purpose.

WEEK 4

1. Last week, we took some time to discuss a few different virtues that can help better ourselves and our school. Who wants to remind the class in their own words what a virtue is? Who remembers the virtues we covered? This week, we will be discussing skills that will help us act on these virtues. These skills are **Communication, Empathy, Emotional Regulation**, and **Social Problem-Solving.** We will also be discussing another virtue that can apply to everything we do, **Positive Purpose**. For those who experienced MCCs last year, can anyone recall what these skills mean or what positive purpose means? Let's start with that. **Positive Purpose** is a virtue that incorporates all of our other virtues, as well as all the skills we will be discussing this week. It is so important for adolescents to develop a sense of purpose, or a deeper meaning of how they can make the world a better place. One way to do that is to consider how you would finish this sentence: "If my life were a book, I would title it …" If you were asked to communicate your purpose, how

would you do it? How does this book title relate to living a positive and purposeful life? What other skills or virtues apply to your title?

2. Today, we have a discussion topic that builds on communication which we talked about yesterday, **Empathy**. Who can define **empathy** for me in their own words (empathy is the understanding and sharing of another's feelings, often accompanied by a desire to help them)? If everyone in school felt empathy for one another, how would this help communication? Can you think of a personal example that would apply?

3. Another skill that is important to be able to act on our virtues is **Emotional Regulation**. For those who learned about MCCs last year, can you recall what **Emotional Regulation** means? This is a skill that is important in order to be a good leader. What would school be like if our principal and administration did not regulate their emotions? Why is this required to be a leader of our school?

4. Today, we will be discussing our final skill, **Social Problem-Solving**. During our MCCs, we will be having a lot of discussions in our classroom with each other, making it a social setting where possible conflict can arise. Keeping our classroom norms in mind, think of an example of how a conflict may arise during MCCs. What can be done to resolve or de-escalate that conflict? What can be done in the future to prevent it from happening again?

5. Everyone did a great job contributing to some very positive conversations this month, while reviewing a lot of important terms in the process! Throughout the rest of the school year, there will be a range of skills and virtues that we will work on during our MCCs. Additionally, we will have a monthly theme to help us maintain some consistency within our conversations (feel free to show a visual like Figure 2.1, if you find it helpful). Some themes come up naturally (e.g., January/Month Three: Planning for the Future) in almost all schools, but we will also use our judgment to see if there is a specific theme worth targeting based on our school. What are some other themes that you think may arise this year?

1. Some of you likely had the opportunity to engage in Morning Classroom Conversations last year and maybe even the year before that. Raise your hand if you remember having MCCs last year! The year before? If you did not have MCCs last year or ever before, there is no need to worry. We will all be exploring year three together! Let's first review what Morning Classroom Conversations are.

   Would anyone who remembers MCCs like to share what they are, for our newcomers? (Based on what is said, use some or all of the following.) This school year, our class will be taking some time each morning to discuss a variety of topics. Some of these topics will be easy to answer and others will make you think deeply. These discussions are going to help us explore our own thoughts and feelings, get to know our class, and practice our skills for discussion and respectful debate, as well as several other skills that are crucial for purposeful living. We will talk more about these skills later this month, but this week we will start by going over classroom norms for our discussions, and engaging in some get-to-know-you questions to warm us up for our Morning Classroom Conversation topics for this school year. Let's discuss some questions I have for you about our MCCs and feel free to ask any of your own questions as well!

   a. Why do you think having regular classroom conversations among classmates in ___ grade is important?

   b. How do conversations help you live a purposeful life at school?

   c. What might be some challenges we will face as a class with these discussions? How can we address these challenges together?

   d. What kinds of questions are you anticipating?

2. Now that we discussed what our morning will be like with the Morning Classroom Conversations, we must also discuss some rules and expectations for these discussions (feel free to involve the class in setting these norms if you wish):

   a. Wait to share your thoughts or answers until it is your turn to speak.

   b. Respect others turn to talk by listening quietly and keeping your answers to a reasonable length.

   c. Be accepting to others' thoughts and ideas—you may share your disagreements thoughtfully and respectfully, when appropriate and/or if time permits.

   d. Use respectful and school-appropriate language.

   e. If you have something to share and did not get to, you may share it with me after class, write it down for our MCC box or submit an MCC Google form.

3. In the first year of MCCs, we played a game called this or that. Some of you may remember. I want you to put your thumb up/down based on

the option that you prefer and after we all signal, we can take turns telling why we picked what we did

- Put your thumb up if you would rather sleep in or thumb down if you prefer to wake up early.
- Music or video games?
- Have someone give you $100 or give $1,000 to a charity of your choice.

WEEK 2

1. This week we are going to practice a few more conversation starters. We will try to do one every day, as a practice for the structure of our MCC. Although these questions may be basic, we are still in our "setting the stage" mode during the month of October (or preparatory month). I hope you are all looking forward to expanding our *Better School* conversations to start the community and world conversations in the month of November/Month One. When was the last time you made someone smile? What was it that made them smile?

2. If you could choose one public place to stay overnight in as a field trip (library, classroom, aquarium, zoo, playground, and mall) what place would you choose?

3. What is most difficult about being a ___ grader?

4. What skill that you have are you most confident you could teach others?

5. If you were asked to invent something and had unlimited resources to do it, what would it be?

WEEK 3

1. Now that we have had a chance to practice with some informal conversation starters, our next couple weeks will review some of the skills and virtues that you learned about in your first and second years of MCCs. Last year, we targeted *Better School*, or how these areas can help create a better school. This year, we will expand by thinking about how these skills and virtues can help develop a better world. Our goal this week is to review important virtues that make our school a better place for everyone. Virtues are part of our character. We will focus on these:

(1) **Optimistic Future-Mindedness;**
(2) **Compassionate Forgiveness and Gratitude;**
(3) **Responsible Diligence;**
(4) **Helpful Generosity;** and
(5) **Constructive Creativity**

Who can recall these virtues from last year? Does anyone remember what they mean?

Let's start by talking about **Optimistic Future-Mindedness**, which means looking toward the future in a hopeful and confident way. What is one thing you are hopeful will positively improve in our country within the next five years? How might your optimistic outlook impact the possibility of this hope becoming a reality? [Discuss the importance of believing in something motivating you to take action.]

2. Today, we are going to talk about **Compassionate Gratitude and Forgiveness.** Social conflict can create tension within a community. If we practice **Compassionate Forgiveness**, we may be better able to work together to improve safety and comfort. What does **Compassionate Forgiveness** mean to you? What would happen in a community group where individuals are not forgiving of other members of that group? [Be sure to mention how communication can't be open if no one is willing to be compassionately forgiving.]

3. **Responsible Diligence** means using careful and persistent effort to take on your duty within a situation. It is our civic responsibility as human beings to create a better world. In order to do so, we all must work together by carefully considering our responsibilities within our community. What types of actions are part of responsible diligence of being a citizen in your community? State? Country? Make your community a better place?

4. Let's talk about **Helpful Generosity**. Thumbs up and thumbs down for this statement: *Everyone should be helping those less fortunate than them.* Why or why not? [Be sure to communicate that by being generous and helping each other, we will have a better world. Also, help does not only need to extend to those who are "less fortunate."]

5. Our last virtue for this week is Constructive Creativity, which means using your imagination in a purposeful way. Not all situations are quickly solved in our country. Name a local or federal leader who you think has used creative ways to make a productive change. What are some persistent problems in your community, in the nation, or in the world that would benefit from constructive creativity to help find solutions?

   Wrap-up of Week 3: Great job with our first set of MCC key concepts this week. Next week, we will introduce the skills we need to act on the virtues and positive purpose.

WEEK 4

1. Last week, we took some time to discuss a few different virtues that can help better ourselves, our school, and our world. Who wants to remind the class in their own words what a virtue is? Who remembers the virtues we covered? This week, we will be discussing skills that will help us act on these virtues. These skills are **Communication**, **Empathy**, **Emotional Regulation**, and **Social Problem-Solving**. We will also be discussing another virtue that can apply to everything we do, **Positive Purpose**. For those who experienced MCCs last year, can anyone recall what these skills mean or what positive purpose means? Let's start by talking about **Positive Purpose**. This virtue incorporates all our other virtues, as well as all of the skills we will be discussing this week. It is so important for adolescents to develop a sense of purpose, or a deeper meaning of how they can make the world a better place. One way to do that is to think about your strengths and **Communicate** how you can improve the world around you. What is one of your biggest strengths or your strongest skill? How can you use this skill to better our world? Be specific in your actions that you can take, even starting today!

2. Today, we have a discussion topic that builds on communication we talked about yesterday, **Empathy**. Who can define **empathy** for me

in their own words (empathy is the understanding and sharing of another's feelings, usually accompanied by a desire to help them)? How might differences within and between cultures make effective communication more difficult? How might empathy help?

3. Another skill that is important to be able to act on our virtues is **Emotional Regulation**. For those who have done MCCs last year, can you recall what **Emotional Regulation** means? **Emotional Regulation** is necessary at a personal, community, and global level. Name a leader who effectively regulates their emotions. How can you tell? How can this skill help create a better world?

4. Today, we will be discussing our final skill, **Social Problem-Solving**. Social conflict can create tension within and between larger communities and even countries around the world. If community members around the world used the virtues we learned last week, we may be able to work together and improve the health and safety of others. What virtue do you think applies the most to this?

5. Everyone did a great job contributing to some very positive conversations this month, while reviewing a lot of important terms in the process! Throughout the rest of the school year, there will be a range of skills and virtues that we will work on during our MCCs. Additionally, we will have a monthly theme to help us maintain some consistency within our conversations (feel free to show a visual like Figure 2.1, if you find it helpful). Some themes come up naturally (e.g., January/Month Three: Planning for the Future) in almost all schools, but we will also use our judgment to see if there is a specific theme worth targeting based on our school. What are some other themes that you think may arise this year?

Chapter Wrap-Up

We anticipate that many students and staff members will be new to the format of classroom conversations or may need a refresher with MCCs. We focused on using "Month Zero" as a time for preparation and practice, in order to help both Conversation Leaders and students become comfortable with the MCC framework. During this preparatory phase, Conversation Leaders explain MCCs, establish norms, foster a productive and safe discussion environment, and introduce key MCC terminology—SEL skills, character virtues, and Positive Purpose—in an engaging and effective way. It's also a good time to work out technological adaptations when using a virtual platform for MCCs.

Reflective Conversations for Growth

Now that you have learned about how to set the foundation for successful MCCs, reflect on/write down the following and commit to taking the appropriate follow-up actions in order to continue to learn and grow as a Conversation Leader.

ACTION STEPS/PRIORITIES

In order to get started on MCCs in November/Month One, what steps could you take to prepare yourself and your students prior to that first formal MCC?

_____

_____

_____

You may be reading this after the second month of your school year, or your intended start period. How might you adapt the MCC sequence to fit your timeline and allow you to introduce and pilot MCCs now toward starting off "on schedule" in the next school year?

_____

_____

_____

CHALLENGES

Although strategies have been provided for preparing your students for MCCs in both Chapters 3 and 4, what other challenges may arise? Who might help you address them?

_____

_____

_____

QUESTIONS

What questions still remain after reading Chapter 4? Are you involved in your local chapter of SEL4US or involved with the national organization? What are others doing to engage their students in SEL-related conversations within their classrooms/teaching contexts?

_____

_____

_____

CHAPTER 5

Guiding a Successful Group Discussion From Start to Finish

As mentioned in earlier chapters, setting a foundation makes it much more likely that you will successfully guide an MCC. Chapter 3 highlighted how to introduce your Morning Classroom Conversations (MCCs), and Chapter 4 highlighted the use of a *preparatory period* to practice MCC skills. Now it's time to begin your own unique journey through MCCs! Of course, many questions lie ahead. How often should these discussions occur? How might the conversations look, depending on the frequency with which you can do this with students, given your role? What are some ways you can keep your students' interest? Read on to learn how to successfully facilitate an MCC from the beginning to the end of the conversation in the context(s) available to you.

 MCC FREQUENCY

MCCs are meant to provide a consistent, safe space for students to socialize, develop skills, and feel connected to each other, the Conversation Leader and the school community. Biologically, cognitively, and socially, youth journey through a metaphorical rollercoaster throughout a given week, even just in one day. With this in mind, having daily conversations is the most powerful model because consistency helps to create clear expectations for students, especially adolescents who may experience every day as having rises and dips and sharp twists and turns. Another analogy is that of vitamins. You don't always feel as if you need them, but by taking them every day, you keep yourself healthier than you would be if you did not. The same goes for MCCs!

SUBJECT-SPECIFIC GROUPS

While it is recommended for MCCs to occur during a homeroom or advisory period, another option is to use MCCs within subject area classes. This would likely occur at the start of that class, followed by a transition from the MCC into academic content, which helps relate the MCC to their lesson in class that day or that week. During pilot programming, this model was especially effective in subjects such as English Language Arts (ELA) and Social Studies. For instance, students understood that when they arrived at their ELA classroom, regardless of what period, there would be an MCC discussion to start the lesson. This served as a kind of verbal "Do Now." Conversation Leaders found it easiest to transition to class content in these particular subject areas, such as targeting the skill of empathy to better relate to the character(s) within the book *The Catcher in the Rye*. That said, transitions are possible in all academic subject areas, including science and mathematics, and special areas, such as music and art. Transition strategies, along with some examples, are discussed in further detail later in this chapter (in the "Concluding Your MCCs" section).

 ## MCCS IN ACTION

The core of MCCs is the set of prompts that start the conversations. Appendices A through C contain what we refer to as the "Full Sequence" document, providing suggested MCC prompts for a daily structure, over a three-year sequence. Other appendices provide guidance for various paths you might take through your own journey of MCCs. Whether you end up creating prompts based on the unique needs of your group or class (as discussed in Chapter 3), using the prompts we provide, or a combination of the two, *how* Conversation Leaders carry out MCCs will strongly determine whether the messages and skill-building opportunities get absorbed by the students.

WHAT ARE SOME WAYS YOU CAN GET YOUR STUDENTS INTERESTED IN MCCS?

Regardless of the structure, many teachers want to know the best way to keep students engaged. Thankfully, adolescent development is a time of advances in thought such as hypothetical thinking, abstract thinking, metacognition, and relative thinking. This means that the level of sophistication among adolescents can allow for a very different conversation than that of children, and we can expect conversations to expand steadily beyond concrete thought. Of course, adolescence is also a time of rapid social cognitive developmental changes such as increases in concern about the perspectives of others, interpersonal relationships, and social norms. These powerful changes must be taken into account during the process of MCC engagement so that instruction is "riding the wave" and not swimming against the current.

Educators have increasingly seen the importance of integrating student voice into standard practice. It's not as if this is a new idea. In the early 1990s, researchers in the United States and internationally began discussing the importance of including student perspectives in discussions (Kozol, 1991; Levin, 1994; Rudduck et al., 1996; Weis & Fine, 1993). By the early 2000s, educators were using the term "student voice" to encourage student concerns to be heard and analyzed, with a problem-solving mindset (Fielding & McGregor, 2005). Research clearly indicates that schools must encourage students to express themselves. Student voice holds the possibility of great transformation among the education system and in this expression, students must feel listened to and understood (Elias, 2010). Educators sometimes forget that the initial step in hearing a student's voice is truly listening, not just hearing. Hence, there is an unappreciated value of simple conversations that can help students to get their day started while also gradually building essential social-emotional competencies students will need in many areas of their lives.

It may seem obvious, but if one is broadcasting the most impressive orchestral music—or any music—with the highest standard of recording and sound encryption possible and the receiver's radio is off, that fantastic music will not be heard. Too often, the metaphorical response to this is to broadcast louder or further improve the quality. Neither of these will matter unless the "on" switch is clicked. Part of the motivation for MCCs is to turn on the learner's "on" switch. The following are some strategies to help be successful in tapping in to students' interests.

MODELING ACTIVE LISTENING

Due to the often untapped potential of emphasizing student voice, one "secret" for successful MCCs is modeling active listening, that is, being sure to communicate to students, both verbally and nonverbally, that you have heard what they said, often by paraphrasing or even by asking if you have understood their point correctly. While actively listening, show kindness and compassion to your students in order to support their journey of character development and encourage their continued participation. MCC Conversation Leaders should maintain eye contact with the speaker, restate what the student shared and utilize conversation enhancers like, "Wow!" "Really? Can you say a little more about that?" or "That's interesting. I did not think that way about it before."

Deeply engage in the discussion so that your students are able to see that you care about what they are saying. Students are sensitive to whether you are fully "present" with your class and this is especially so during MCCs whose purpose is to give students' words attention and focus. During this time, it may be tempting to move around the room to finish up your last minutes of preparations, but this is highly discouraged because it creates the assumption that your preparation is more important than what your students have to say.

ENSURING STUDENTS LISTEN AND RESPOND TO ONE ANOTHER

Similar to how your own active listening shows students that what they are saying is important to you, a key role of Conversation Leaders is to help students feel supported by their peers. As noted in Chapter 3, MCC norms establish a climate of mutual respect and the importance of listening. The next step is to promote engaging exchanges among peers, and the Conversation Leader can do this by encouraging students to comment on one another's responses in respectful, genuine, inquiring ways. Creating that expectation, modeling and guiding students in how to make those responses will draw students into the conversations. Remember, this is a learning process; it's not as if this is a skill all students have. However, once they come to realize that their goal is not to simply wait for their turn to speak and be finished with the conversation after that, students' engagement increases. Why? They find that comments from their peers are as valued, and valuable, as their own thoughts. You can begin to see the potent way in which this conversation format builds social-emotional learning (SEL) muscles and shapes virtues. If you notice that many students seem disconnected, it is suggested that the Conversation Leader(s) review the group norms and empower students to problem solve about how to engage the group as a whole. If a particular student still appears disengaged, it may be beneficial to pull them aside to discuss ways to demonstrate active listening or explore other barriers to engagement.

CREATING STUDENT SUBCOMMITTEES

To take empowerment a step further, one suggestion is to create a student subcommittee to assist with generating MCC topics/prompts. This subcommittee should reflect the diversity in the class, by gender, ethnicity, language, and ability/disability. Most of the MCC prompts are pre-established, so consider the idea of having one of the MCCs each week to be student-generated topics. The goal would be to empower the committee to speak with classmates to generate ideas and propose them to the Conversation Leader for the day assigned to student-generated topics. Note that there can be empowerment within a structure; that is, you can give students a focus (e.g., a skill like empathy and perspective taking or a virtue like Optimistic Future-Mindedness, or any focal skill or virtue your classroom or school is working on) and have students generate various aspects they would like to have conversations about.

GENERAL TIPS AND STRATEGIES TO FOSTER CONVERSATIONS

As topics are predetermined with the student voice in mind, it is unlikely that students will lack interest in the conversation completely. With that being said, there is a possibility that some topics will not spark in-depth discussion, so here are some tips for how to keep your MCCs flowing in such circumstances.

ALLOW FOR SILENCE

While silence may be uncomfortable for a few seconds, it can create space to process and allow students to come up with new ideas. More often than not, if enough silent space is given, a student will speak out to the group. Even if it might feel unusual in the beginning, students (and Conversation Leaders alike) will begin to embrace the silence to allow for productive thought. Indeed, you might find it useful to say, "I think it's often helpful to take a minute or two in silence—which usually feels a lot longer—to gather my thoughts when I am considering a new or challenging question. You may find the same thing to be true for you."

ASK FOLLOW-UP QUESTIONS

There is a surprising power in questions (Brooks & John, 2018). Almost all MCCs are open-ended questions, intentionally. In trying to create a space for new information to be shared, these questions will allow for a discussion without limiting that information to a series of responses or a simple "yes" or "no" response. These types of questions do not have one correct answer but rather reinforce the idea that there are different views on a set of beliefs that can be equally valid. It is important to consider when to ask another open-ended question, when to use a question with structured responses, and when to sustain the silence. For instance, if the room seems particularly tense, an open-ended question may provoke more stress than productivity so it may make sense to take a poll of the room using a question like, "Who agrees with this statement?" and asking some students to share why, before moving on. Other effective follow-up questions include "Who will add to what Julio said?" "Akirra, is there something different you would like to talk about? Do you have a question you would like us to think about and discuss?" and "Komal, what did you hear Pat say, and what is your own answer to the question?"

Some MCCs will not last for the suggested 10- to 15-minute time frame. For instance, let's consider some of the shorter MCCs that will be presented in the Full Sequence document:

1. *Finish the sentence: "I care a lot about _____. I think all middle school students should be able to _____."*

When considering how one might engage students through an MCC with such a short prompt, the Conversation Leader may decide to have the entire class/group complete the sentence. Alternatively, Conversation Leaders may preface an MCC of this kind by saying, "Today we are going to work in small groups. I want you to think about why you might answer questions the same way or differently." By allowing for discussion within groups and then sharing out, students are not only self-reflective but also able to explore how their answers may differ or relate to those of others in the class. Pair-share and small group discussions with sharing out are useful ways to extend conversations based on shorter prompts.

2. *Pick three words that describe you.*

If this is introduced as a group discussion, students may be encouraged to ask follow-up questions to the responses. For instance, the Conversation Leader may give the example "Why did you choose the word 'trustworthy' to describe yourself? Tell me a time you kept someone's trust." This would encourage students to ask follow-up questions to their peers, instead of a quick three-word response. For this prompt, rather than opening a discussion to the class, the Conversation Leader may decide to have students engage in a pair and share immediately after receiving this prompt. Students could compare similarities and differences, like the group example earlier, or explore how different people in their lives might describe them.

USE HUMOR

Everyone enjoys a good laugh. Rebecca Alber (2015) wrote a popular blog called 20 *Tips for Creating a Safe Learning Environment*. She stated, "Learning doesn't have to always be so serious, nor do we. Sometimes, when tensions are high … we need to laugh together. It's okay" (para. 17). Not only is it okay, but it is also considered to be a positive attribute for teachers and allows students to have a sense of humor within the classroom. Although MCCs may lead to deep conversations, you also need to find appropriate moments to lighten the mood and joke with your students. One Conversation Leader during pilot programming had the questions on an index card, and when it was met by sustained silence, she ripped it up and flamboyantly threw it away and said that she did not want to make the mistake of ever using that awful question again. That broke the tension in the group, and she gave students a choice of where the conversation could go next.

TALK DIRECTLY ABOUT THE DISCOMFORT

It may be helpful to talk directly about what is different about a particular MCC that doesn't seem to spark group interest. Ask questions like "I notice the group is a bit quieter today. Who wants to try to tackle the elephant in the room?" or "What makes this prompt harder to discuss than others?" Some MCCs are not a great fit for a particular class of students—you will know this relative to your own students better than anyone else—and that is okay! Rather than pushing the conversation to continue, the MCC could shift into a reflection of the question and its challenges, which may be even more productive than the expected conversation following the original MCC prompt.

LET THE STUDENTS LEAD

Beyond the aforementioned suggestion of allowing students to come up with MCC topics, some Conversation Leaders may decide to allow students to lead the conversation for a day. In the pilot schools, through a youth leadership program, some students were given the opportunity to facilitate discussions within their homeroom class. More specifically, some classes elected student ambassadors, among whose responsibilities included being given the opportunity to lead classroom conversations (with some preparation, of course), and this was observed to be effective (Hatchimonji et al., 2017; Murphy et al., 2020). Rotating students, along with educators, in posing or creating questions and leading discussions deepens investment in the activity. Beyond the classroom, the MCC can take engagement a step further by providing an opportunity for older students to facilitate the conversations for younger students within the same school. This approach can be particularly effective when students are in their second or third year of MCCs.

 ## CONCLUDING YOUR MCCS

HOW DO YOU BRING THE SHORT YET SOCIALLY AND EMOTIONALLY RICH MCCS TO A CLOSE?

Overall, flexibility is key to see success here! Instructors, group leaders, and clinicians always have to be mindful of the clock alongside the integrity of the activity they are engaging in. In this way, MCCs are no different from teaching or therapy. Bringing conversations to an appropriate closure, not ending abruptly, and pointing to when a conversation in progress will be able to be completed constitute best practices.

In a way, particularly when MCCs go well, it can be a challenge to wrap them up and move into the subject area students have next, whether math, language arts, physical education, or music. Sometimes, teachers feel as though conversations would benefit from more time than the 10 to 15 minutes allotted. Adhering to the schedule limits actually builds essential social-emotional competencies such as the following:

- *Delay of gratification*: School and many things in life are based on the clock. It is necessary to get used to not having all the time one would ideally want to say or do what one wishes, even if important. This is one reason why having a predictable schedule for MCC is so valuable. Students will come to learn that they will have a chance to speak next time. Don't hesitate to revisit a particularly engaging conversation the next day. That's why it often is helpful to be clear with students when the conversation will be picked up once again. A related skill-builder for delay of gratification is to create a clear number of "sharers" during each MCC. In other words, it is not realistic for all students to share in each conversation, so if there is an understood number of people who can share, then the students will know when the conversation, or a given portion of a conversation, has ended. In using this strategy, be sure to rotate the people who are given the opportunity to share. For instance, if ten students have an idea but the teacher almost always chooses Kai, Angela, and Crystal first, this will discourage other students from sharing.

- *Social problem-solving*: If time is expiring and students have something they feel they must communicate before the next MCC time, they can problem solve how best to do this. Conversation Leaders can discuss this explicitly when introducing MCC to the students. If the message is directed toward the Conversation Leader, the task is to problem solve when and how to communicate this appropriately. If the follow-up is with a classmate, similarly, some thinking about when, where, and how to do this in the short term can be good exercise of students' problem-solving skills. And, of course, their analysis could yield the conclusion that it is just best to wait until the next opportunity, or perhaps what they were concerned about was not so essential to convey. Some ideas during piloting included an MCC box, special MCC email address, or arranging to stay after class when the issue is urgent. Chapter 3 reviews specific pre-MCC preparation that would ensure a crisis protocol is in place, if needed.

- *Reflection and planning*: Encourage students to review their patterns of participation (and help them do this when necessary). Are they finding they are waiting too long to participate and hence often get to the end without expressing a thought they wanted to share? Are they hesitant to know how to get the attention of the Conversation Leader so that they can be recognized to participate? Conversation Leaders can open the door for students to follow up with them if they are finding themselves challenged to participate as they wish. Some students may prefer a format other than open class discussion, so consider also using pair-share, small-group discussions, and other mechanisms, such as putting responses on sticky notes, putting them up on a board, and then sorting them into common themes, to ensure that wide student participation is in place so that more students are able to voice their views than would happen if only one-speaker-at-a-time discussion formats were used. You may find that creating a self-reflection rubric students can use to periodically evaluate their own participation and set goals for improvement will operationalize the preceding points well.

CORE CONTENT TRANSITIONING STATEMENTS

For those Conversation Leaders who are leading MCCs before a core content area (e.g., homeroom teachers who remain with their students into the first block or period of the day), it will be important to prepare for the transition into content area classes once the 10 to 15 minutes of MCCs is up. When conversations are ended without transition, it is more likely that students will struggle to shift their focus and may become distracted by not understanding the continuity between MCCs and their next classes. Of course, this is not an issue unique to MCCs; the schedule of the day for most secondary students is replete with discontinuity. From a social-emotional character development (SECD) perspective, it is important to not play into this but rather to alleviate it. Furthermore, without a smooth and sensible transition into core content, students may have trouble generalizing the skills and takeaways brought about by the MCCs, which may hinder the many benefits that SECD bring.

We find that the best strategy is to take advantage of the flexibility provided by the MCC sample prompts for each given month and provide transition statements such as the following examples be used whenever possible following MCCs, which may require some mental preparation and creativity prior to each MCC in your classroom. Remember, that you can recall recent MCCs, as well as those immediately proximal to your lesson. Some examples of transition statements linked to prompts for various subject areas follow:

- *Math*: Our conversation today targeted the importance of thinking about the past in order to pave the way for the future, how might this apply to our lesson in math today? Think about all of the things you have learned in math up until this year! How have prior skills that we've learned built upon each other to apply to our current lesson?

- *Writing*: Going along with our discussion this morning about organization, why might this skill be just as important with writing as it is with other areas of your life? What does it mean to be organized when you are writing?

- *Reading*: Thinking about heroes, we are going to transition into our literature review from last night. Who do you think the main character in our book would label as their hero?

- *Social Studies*: Throughout history, as long as there have been human beings, individuals had a wide variety of feelings. Today, we are going to talk about Martin Luther King, Jr. and I want you to think about how he might have responded to our MCC.

- *Science*: Scientists need to persevere through many experiments before finding the appropriate solution. Today, we are going to do a lab that may be a little challenging for you, but I want you to keep pushing forward despite the challenge. What are some strategies for dealing with setbacks that you have heard about in our MCCs?

- *Special Areas* [e.g., Music/Art/Physical Education]: Let's apply today's discussion on positivity to our [singing/drawing/game] during today's class. What activity that you might have been having some trouble with will you try to approach today with confidence? How can you help yourself and your classmates/teammates/groupmates be more confident?

For Conversation Leaders outside of the suggested MCC structure, such as a school counselors holding a weekly group and using MCCs to open the group, transition statements are valuable when concluding your group and sending students back to class. This can be done by taking two to three minutes at the conclusion of your session to ask students what they are learning in their next class and brainstorm together how your MCC that day may apply to their next activity.

HOW DO YOU TELL IF YOUR MCCS ARE EFFECTIVE FOR STUDENTS AND IF YOU'RE SUCCESSFUL AS A CONVERSATION LEADER?

With the MCC format being new to you as an educator and new to your students, you may be concerned as to how to tell if your students are experiencing success with MCCs, the same way they would show success and understanding in homework assignments or unit tests. When introducing MCCs, there is no formal evaluation to track progress, but the best way to know that your students are benefiting from these conversations is the way in which they interact with one another and the level of awareness and understanding they have of their own actions.

In Chapter 1, the use of student self-reflective rubrics was mentioned. This will help you gauge the level of insight they are getting from their conversations. You also will be able to note potential discrepancies between how students see themselves and what their actions communicate. Those discrepancies should trigger important conversations between you and the student, with the goal of planning specific actions and observations that seem indicated to reduce the discrepancies.

Relatedly, your observation of the impact of MCCs on your students is vital in guiding your efforts, both during the introductory period and throughout the year. Based on these observations, you can address any setbacks or modifications needed to better suit your group of students. You might assess the confidence of the group or ask questions such as "Are your students getting along better during class?" If you are looking for a more specific way to assess the impact of MCCs, especially relating to virtues, it is suggested to utilize the Outcomes of MCCs rubric in Appendix D. This unique tool allows you to monitor progress in a concrete, measurable way.

These are just some of the many instances that your students are likely to show noticeable improvement with in just a short time through active engagement in MCCs.

Chapter Wrap-Up

You are now aware of everything needed to start an MCC all the way through to wrapping up the conversation. We covered the frequency and duration of discussions along with specific techniques, such as modeling active listening, that support student engagement and foster effective conversation. We concluded with how to wrap up MCCs in an effective, timely way and transition students to their next school activity, all while keeping in mind that this is a learning experience for both students and Conversation Leaders. In reviewing the transition, subject-specific statements were provided as a model. Last, in an effort to help you track the effectiveness of your MCCs, a progress monitoring rubric was introduced.

Reflective Conversations for Growth

Now that you have reviewed the basic strategies for facilitating an MCC from start to finish, reflect on/write down the following and commit to taking the appropriate follow-up actions in order to continue to learn and grow as a Conversation Leader.

ACTION STEPS/PRIORITIES

Knowing the students in your class/group and based on any practice period you already have had, what might you need to do first in order to ensure engagement/buy-in among your students?

_____

_____

_____

ADAPTATIONS

Do you think you will need to adapt MCCs outside the daily MCC structure (suggested daily 10–15 minutes)? Think creatively, what type of adaptation might be appropriate? If you are stuck, the following chapter will review options for alternative implementation models.

_____

_____

_____

CHALLENGES

Do you suspect that your MCCs will run over time? What do you plan to do to monitor the timing of your discussions? Is there anything you might need to do to appropriately prepare for this challenge?

_____

_____

_____

QUESTIONS

What questions still remain after reading Chapter 5? If you're concerned about student engagement or how to have a smooth integration of our SEL program into your current class structure, consider submitting questions and/or comments to the

Social-Emotional Learning Alliance for the United States (SEL4US), and/or your state SEL4US affiliate. Also, feel free to visit our web page to read our responses to what other teachers have asked.

_____

_____

_____

CHAPTER 6

Alternative Implementation Options

While the approach to Morning Classroom Conversations (MCCs) discussed thus far will be well matched to most circumstances, for others there will be a need to adapt the procedure to meet particular needs of certain groups, classes, or schools. There may be a need for guiding successful MCCs within a different context (e.g., during math class), using a less frequent structure, such as three times a week, or intervening with a targeted group over a short time. If this is the case, it is imperative for the Conversation Leader(s) and their students to clearly establish a regular and predictable schedule for the MCCs. Indeed, throughout your experience with MCCs, you must be systematic if you want to see systematic results. In whichever of the following contexts you find yourself, create a routine and a schedule that you can (largely) stick to. Of course, it's appropriate to experiment a bit before you settle on an approach—you don't want the perfect to be the enemy of the good! With that framing in mind, you can consider the alternative implementation models in this chapter most realistically.

 REGULAR, NON-DAILY CONVERSATIONS

Indeed, during pilot work, some teachers expressed concern with a daily model. Some common barriers included high demands of curriculum content, desire to achieve more academic goals, and varied student arrival times. Sometimes, teachers want to ease their way in, to get a handle on what MCCs involve, and then turn to a five-day format. It is quite possible that these barriers exist for you, as well, and flexibility will be required in order to make the MCCs work for your classroom community. One example encountered was a program called "Breakfast Before the Bell," during which time breakfast was served during homeroom or advisory. At first, students needed to get accustomed to the quick breakfast routine and were not eager to engage in any conversations, let alone MCCs. However, after a week or two, they adapted to the breakfast routine and MCC participation increased. It's not an ideal situation, to be sure, but it's quite feasible. Creativity is encouraged, and at times, administrative buy-in will be needed in order to formulate the appropriate implementation model for your classroom. Here are some alternate, workable models that occur on a less frequent basis.

THREE TIMES PER WEEK

Rather than having MCCs when time permits, it is more effective to have an MCC scheduled for a certain number of times per week during homeroom. The predictability of this structure will create more successful discussions, as students come to anticipate the timing and organization of MCCs. For example, it is more productive if students understand that on Monday, Wednesday, and Friday, the MCCs will be the first activity of their day than if they arrive each day wondering if an MCC will be occurring.

Regardless of the days of the week you pick, some minor decisions, such as which prompts to prioritize, will need to be made. As the Full Sequence provides five prompts each week, it is suggested that you use your own professional opinion and discretion to determine which prompts are most appropriate. All prompts are written to be "free-standing," that is, so there is no reference to "yesterday" or "tomorrow." This was done intentionally to allow for flexibility during days that the school is closed for a state or national holiday or schedules are changed for staff professional development or the myriad of reasons why a Conversation Leader may not be able to make it to all five prompts in a given week.

In order to paint a picture of the selection process, let's take a sample week from December/Month Two in Year 1 (*Better Me*) and explore the opportunities for choosing three prompts (see Table 6.1).

TABLE 6.1 ● December/Month Two in Year 1 (*Better Me*)

	MONDAY	TUESDAY	WEDNESDAY	THURSDAY	FRIDAY
Dec. Week 1	Is it easier or harder to understand what someone means when texting? Have you ever had someone misinterpret your words in a text? Do you prefer to text, call, video chat, or speak in person? Why? (Skill: Communication)	Name one thing that someone gave you that matters to you. Why does this item (or action) matter to you? (Virtue: Helpful Generosity)	When you find yourself facing a problem, how do you try to solve it? How do you think things through? How did you learn how to do this? (Skill: Social Problem-Solving)	What is your body language saying right now? How might I know by looking at you if you were actively engaged in the discussion? Once you think about it, is there anything you would want to change? (Skill: Communication)	Think of one thing or object that you really love: maybe your house, your pet, or your phone. What would you do if you were without that thing? How would your life be different? (Theme: Giving Back to Ourselves, School and World)

In looking at these prompts, there are two questions targeting the skill of communication; as a Conversation Leader, you would likely choose one of those, a question targeting a virtue and a question targeting the theme of the month. Others might decide to focus on communication more than once if they know this is a skill for which their students need support. If the same theme was addressed the week prior, a Conversation Leader could look to target virtues and skills in the second week. These choices really are determined by your professional judgment, based on the circumstances you are facing.

ONE TIME PER WEEK

Some teachers use consistent "MCC Mondays," with an understanding that there will not be another MCC until next week. While this reduces the amount of practice students get exercising their SEL and conversational muscles, it will better support your students than having no MCCs or spontaneous conversations when there appears to be extra time. One way is to follow a monthly format that teaches a series of skills and utilizes virtues, targeting an overall theme. For instance, the month might look something like Table 6.2.

TABLE 6.2 ● January/Month Three (Year 1—*Better Me*): Planning for the Future

	MCC WEEKLY PROMPT
Week 1	A new student just arrived at your school. What do you think it feels like to be living in a new place with all new people? Has this happened to you? (Skill: Empathy)
Week 2	If we disagree with someone's perspective, what would be the best thing to do? Have you ever had trouble doing this? (Skill: Social Problem-Solving)
Week 3	Small miracles happen every day. What could you do to raise your awareness of these miracles? (Virtue: Optimistic Future-Mindedness)
Week 4	What do you like most about being a _____ grader? When do you feel you are at your best in the school? (Virtue: Optimistic Future-Mindedness)

It is also possible that you are facilitating prompts once per week but are able to allocate more time (e.g., a half hour), so you might want to introduce two prompts per session and adjust the format accordingly. Table 6.3 shows how you might select prompts for that particular structure.

TABLE 6.3 ● January/Month Three (Year 1—*Better Me*): Planning for the Future

	MCC WEEKLY PROMPT 1	MCC WEEKLY PROMPT 2
Week 1	A new student just arrived at your school. What do you think it feels like to be living in a new place with all new people? Has this happened to you? (Skill: Empathy)	"Don't judge others unless you are standing in their shoes." Do you agree with that quote? What does it have to do with empathy? (Skill: Empathy)
Week 2	If we disagree with someone's perspective, what would be the best thing to do? Have you ever had trouble doing this? (Skill: Social Problem-Solving)	What is it like to work in a group where others do not communicate effectively to solve a problem? (Skill: Social Problem-Solving)
Week 3	Small miracles happen every day. What could you do to raise your awareness of these miracles? (Virtue: Optimistic Future-Mindedness)	Pessimism has been related to stress, anxiety, and depression. What could you do today to help combat your negative thoughts and turn them into positive thoughts? (Virtue: Optimistic Future-Mindedness)
Week 4	What do you like most about being a _____ grader? When do you feel you are at your best in the school? (Virtue: Optimistic Future-Mindedness)	What is something about your future that you are optimistic about? Why? (Virtue: Optimistic Future-Mindedness)

The two-prompt structure allows a group to have a deeper conversation about a skill (e.g., empathy) by the Conversation Leader asking two questions and allowing more time to reflect on the prompt. Additionally, if a conversation is going well, this structure allows more participants to be involved in the conversation rather than the time constraints limiting to a certain number of responses (i.e., only using one prompt, if appropriate). As Table 6.3 delineates, it is recommended to have both prompts within a given week have the same focus, whether that be a skill or a virtue.

Conversation Leaders can create alternate structures based on perception of students' needs. For example, one month might emphasize skills and virtues; another month might emphasize virtues and themes; a third month might employ prompts for skills and themes. These three-month cycles can then be repeated. If you are in a secondary school with a six-day schedule, or Red and Blue days, and so on, feel free to accommodate this schedule. For example, you might have MCCs only on Blue days; you might have them once every six days; or you might have them on days 1 and 6. The key is to have a regular, predictable schedule. This allows for both your planning prompts systematically and for your students to know when they will be having their conversation opportunities—to which they will be increasingly looking forward.

SHORT-TERM SMALL GROUPS/ EXTRACURRICULAR ACTIVITIES

Often, school mental health professionals and out-of-school program providers have an opportunity to run time-limited small groups of students in need of behavioral, emotional, or social skills development. MCCs can be helpful openers for these meetings. Elias and Tobias (2018) discuss how school counselors, in particular, find themselves in this kind of situation. There is a temptation to try to cover all the areas in which students have needs, but most often, this results in superficial understanding of multiple areas. They recommend that the groups focus on skills (or virtues, though likely not as often, as skills tend to be a higher priority for students in these groups). Your MCC openers for the group might follow the skill-based format depicted in Table 6.4.

TABLE 6.4 ● Skill: Social Problem-Solving and Communication

	MCC PROMPT
Session 1	Our group will be taking about 15 minutes at the start of each group to discuss a variety of topics. Some of these topics will be easy to answer and others will make you think deeply. These discussions are going to help us explore our own thoughts and feelings, get to know our group, practice our skills for discussion and respectful debate, as well as several other skills that are crucial for purposeful living. Today, we will start by discussing some rules and expectations for these discussions (the following norms are suggestions that can be adjusted to fit your group, added to your existing norms, etc.): 1. Wait to share your thoughts or answers until it is your turn to speak. 2. Respect others turn to talk by listening quietly and keeping your answers to a reasonable length. 3. Be accepting to others' thoughts and ideas—you may share your disagreements thoughtfully and respectfully, when appropriate and/or if time permits. 4. Use respectful and school-appropriate language. 5. If you have something to share and did not get to, you may share it with me after group, write it down for our MCC box or submit an MCC Google form.
Session 2	Today, we are going to do a self-assessment of our strengths and aspects of our behavior we might want to improve. Take out a piece of paper (or go around the room, dependent on group size) and list at least three personal strengths. How might these strengths impact your success in the group this year? Now, name one area about yourself that you would like to improve. What is something that you will do to be aware of this throughout the group?
Session 3	Describe a time you learned to think about a problem in a new way (with Constructive Creativity). Did anyone help you think in a new way? (Skill: Social Problem-Solving)
Session 4	Can you think of a time you were honest even though it was hard? Have you ever told a harmless lie, just to spare someone else's feelings? Just about everyone has. Does that make you dishonest? (Skill: Communication)
Session 5	Is it helpful to be positive all the time? Why or why not? (Skill: Social Problem-Solving)
Session 6	If you were to make a playlist with songs that fit your personality and best describe you, what songs would you choose? Why? (Skill: Communication)
Session 7	Discuss how to use "pros and cons" for real-life decision-making using hypothetical situations. Ask students to do the same about a decision they are currently making. (Skill: Social Problem-Solving)
Session 8	What question(s) do you still have about middle school/high school? What can you do to seek answers to the question(s)? (Skill: Communication)
Session 9	If you were given $1 million, how would you use it to make yourself, school, or world better? (Skill: Social Problem-Solving)
Session 10	If you could only use 10 words to describe what is most important in your life, what would they be? [Consider having all students write their answer to this question and then work in small groups to see if any words on the list were the same] (Skill: Communication) *Note:* You might want to substitute a revisiting of Session 2 if this were not a focus of this last session, asking students to reflect on areas in which they grew from strength and improved in areas of need.

In this suggested format, the MCC prompt would introduce the skill for each session, and then the group activity or activities for the day would focus on skill development. The unfolding sequence of themes provide a natural progression for the group over 10 sessions, with the first two sessions being directed toward building trust, group cohesion, and participants' understanding and sharing what they need to work on and the strengths they have to bring to the process. As the group progresses, the skills of social problem-solving and communication are continuously targeted throughout sessions 3 to 10. If you take a look at the Full Sequence (see Appendix A), you will note that all prompts within this chart are from the month of November/Month One in Year 1. These skills are also paired within the months of December/ Month Two and May/Month Seven, so those prompts can be used, as well as those from Year 2 and/or Year 3. As mentioned, use your professional judgment and knowledge of your students and situation to pick the prompts you think are best; the examples include plenty of prompts for each skill.

Often, the time limit for groups might be six sessions, and the way school life is configured, it is likely those sessions will take place over more than six weeks. This makes it easy for participants to lose the thread of what the group is trying to accomplish. In such cases, focusing on one particular skill, such as empathy, is likely to have the most enduring impact. You might want to start the group each session with one of the many prompts targeting the skill of Empathy and Perspective Taking, and if you look at January/Month Three, March/Month Five, and April/Month Six, you will find that these are the targeted skills. Conversation Leaders may, on the MCC website, search specific terms from the Full Sequence documents using the Control + F function that will allow you to organize MCC prompts by skill. It is highly recommended to use this feature to develop prompts for each session.

EXTRACURRICULAR ACTIVITIES

Rather than engaging in MCCs during the school day, you may be a club facilitator who sees a need for improving SEL via conversation within your extracurricular activity. If you are running an after-school group (e.g., "Teen Social," "Service Club," and "Student Council") or an out-of-school group (e.g., YM/YWCA, Girl or Boy Scouts, and camping groups), you might benefit from having MCCs within the structure. As it is likely that the group runs once per week, you can potentially use the once-weekly structure to facilitate MCCs throughout the entire life of the group.

Students Against Destructive Decisions (SADD) is an example of a club that may benefit from considering the monthly themes in order to target different issues across the school. For instance, when the club begins (let's say, for this example, an October start) you can have the students brainstorm ways to target the theme, "What Kind of Person Do I Want to Be?" Students may engage in self-reflection activities to think about ways to improve their self-concept using journaling, prompt completion, and/or gratitude exercises. If this is a club that targets school-based problem-solving, it may be beneficial to consider how to improve self-image on a more global scale with schoolwide initiatives, such as putting sticky notes with quotes like "Shine On" and "Smile, You Look Great" on bathroom mirrors. The same type of activity can continue monthly using the MCC themes:

1. *November/Month One:* Making Ourselves, School, and World Better

2. *December/Month Two:* Giving Back to Ourselves, School, and World

3. *January/Month Three:* Planning for the Future

4. *February/Month Four:* Showing Resilience and Overcoming Obstacles

5. *March/Month Five:* Appreciating Ourselves, Our School, and the World

6. *April/Month Six:* Connecting With Others and Being a Leader

7. *May/Month Seven:* Looking Forward: Next Steps on the Journey

8. *June/Month Eight:* Looking Back: What Have I Accomplished? What Have I Learned?

The most popular extracurricular activity in the United States is athletics. Whether you coach the lacrosse team, cheerleading team, or surfing club, there is a way to embed MCCs within your practices. Unified Champion Schools, an inclusive athletics program initiated by Special Olympics, uses a version of MCCs to open many of their team meetings and practice sessions. Similar to the structure for small groups mentioned earlier, find a skill or virtue, choose prompts that stick out to you and seem to match your team's developmental progression and start one practice a week with a prompt.

LUNCH GROUPS AS A SPECIAL CASE

Many school professionals find that one opportunity to work with students on social-emotional matters is through lunch groups. The reasons are obvious—these groups do not interfere with the students' usual schedule, and lunch often does not seem like a productive use of time, otherwise. Of course, from the students' perspective, things usually look a little different. Lunch is a respite for many of them and is a relatively unstructured, low-pressure time to which they look forward. It has been found (Gale et al., 2017) that lunch groups are not a time to require serious focus or deep exploration on the part of students. Indeed, the kind of gentle skill building that MCCs provide can be an ideal structure for a series of time-limited lunch groups that also allow for preservation of that highly valued time for respite.

For this model, it is recommended to start with the *Better School* or *Better World* foci, as they fit well with a lunch group format. They are externally focused and can lead students to de-center from themselves a bit, which is especially important in adolescence. Sometimes, it's a relief to think about others and to find oneself in a helping mode. After starting the group by setting ground rules and expectations, pick one or two related virtues, like Generosity and Optimistic Future-Mindedness, or two related skills, Empathy and Social Problem-Solving or Empathy and Communication, as your focus. Next, you can use the master list of prompts (Appendices A–C or at the MCC website) to select two prompts per meeting that your students will discuss, similar to the sample in Table 6.5.

TABLE 6.5 ● Sample of Seven-Week Lunch Group

MCC PROMPTS (OPTIMISTIC FUTURE-MINDEDNESS)	MCC PROMPTS (HELPFUL GENEROSITY)
Students are under a lot of pressure. What could you do to make a friend at school smile later today? What about an adult in the school? *(Better School)*	"No one can help everyone, but everyone can help someone." What do you think about this quote? How can it apply to our school? *(Better School)*
Every school has some bad or sad things happen. What can you remember that was bad or sad that happened in this school or a school you were in? How did the school improve as a result, even though it was hard? *(Better School)*	Who in this school comes to mind when I say the word "goodness"? What makes this person good? What qualities do you have that others may think remind them of "goodness"? *(Better School)*
Every school has potential to be better. What can make this school better from now to the end of the school year? What do you look forward to in your next grade level or school? *(Better School)*	Think about a hero or heroine in social studies or history that you have studied in this school. What made this person heroic? Do you consider anyone in the school to be a hero or heroine? *(Better School)*
What is one positive thing that you have done for others this week? How does that help make the world a better place? *(Better World)*	Do you expect people to be generous to you? Why or why not? Should people expect you to be generous to them? *(Better World)*
On any news network, we learn so much about the bad events occurring around the world. If you could say one sentence to a news reporter about optimistic future-mindedness, what would you tell them? *(Better World)*	Men and women volunteer in our country to be a part of the military. What do you think motivates them to do this? *(Better World)*
What are some mental health benefits of feeling comfortable with people from different races, backgrounds, abilities, etc.? *(Better World)*	"The happiest people are the givers, not the getters." Do you agree or disagree? Why? *(Better World)*

Chapter Wrap-Up

For any program to work in a school over time, it has to be adaptable, and that is certainly true for MCCs. While it is optimal to have MCCs daily and at the start of a student's day, we understand that this may not always be possible. We provided samples of different kinds of adaptations that have been made and we encourage your creative brainstorming to determine how MCCs can be adapted to best meet the needs of your students. One caveat: we highly discourage random MCCs, as some level of continuity is what creates a climate of safety and collaboration which will lead to more fruitful discussions and progressive skill building. Regardless of what it looks like, providing structure and consistency is the key to success!

Reflective Conversations for Growth

Now that you have familiarized yourself with a few of the many alternative options for MCCs, reflect on/write down the following and commit to taking the appropriate follow-up actions in order to continue to learn and grow as a Conversation Leader.

ACTION STEPS/PRIORITIES

What alternative option, if any, are you considering for your MCC group? What will you need to do to prepare for this option?

_____

_____

_____

ADAPTATIONS

If you are not carrying out a daily approach, how might you supplement students' MCC experiences by integrating MCCs into existing academic/specials classes and/or creating throughlines in those classes from the MCCs you do implement?

_____

_____

_____

CHALLENGES

What is one challenge you foresee with implementing this alternative framework? How can you address this challenge? Who can help?

_____

_____

_____

QUESTIONS

What questions still remain after reading Chapter 6? Consider submitting one or two questions to the authors at MorningClassroomConversations@gmail.com.

_____

_____

_____

CHAPTER 7

Individualizing Your Morning Classroom Conversations

Differentiated instruction, personalized learning, and educational equity—all these terms and others have been used over the years to recognize that students learn at different rates and in different ways. As Morning Classroom Conversations (MCCs) are meant to be accessible to all students, it is important to consider how to ensure their appropriateness for students with varying abilities and English language learners (ELLs) and to be sensitive to cultural differences and a wide variety of learning preferences. This chapter highlights some tips and strategies to consider when individualizing MCCs to match your learners.

HOW DO YOU ADDRESS DIFFERING COGNITIVE LEVELS?

As educators, you specialize in tailoring instruction to the unique individual needs of students. That is why effective MCC individualization should be approached as you would approach any other lesson within your class or group. If, for example, you were about to present a mathematics lesson or a social studies debate, how would you address the differing cognitive levels among your students? Consider applying these changes to match a conversational format.

Your class may include a wide range of cognitive levels, so the best way to introduce each MCC is to use a multimodal format. Keep the prompt concise and to the point, providing further clarification, if needed. It may be beneficial to write the MCC prompt on the board, project it digitally, verbally present it, and ask a student to put the question in their own words. Strategies like these not only allow access for both visual and auditory learners, but if a student has weak reading comprehension skills or struggles to process auditory information, the multimodal presentation allows an opportunity for a style that they might find more comfortable.

Special educators should review the prompts prior to implementation and consider modifications and/or accommodations that would best assist their students. Piloting of MCCs has indicated that these conversations can be appropriate and fruitful for all students, including those that receive pullout support and those who are in inclusion or self-contained classes. In fact, within an inclusion setting or those classes that involve both general education and special education students, MCCs allow a unique opportunity for all students, including those that may struggle academically, to thrive. As these discussions draw more upon everyday life skills and awareness and less on subject area content, those students who may shy away from participating in an academic lesson may be more comfortable joining an MCC.

When introducing general education and special education students to MCCs within an inclusive setting, it is expected that the general education teacher would introduce the prompt and the special education teacher would follow-up using the necessary accommodations, which would consist of variations or alternative formats available to all students. For instance, consider the prompt "When do you feel bored? What are all the ways you have dealt with being bored? What other ideas might work?" as a sample. The general education teacher would say this prompt to the entire class, often repeating it twice to ensure everyone heard the questions. The special education teacher, as they would do with any other verbally presented information, may want to convey it in written form for the students, such as visually presenting each question in a numbered list or paraphrase by saying, as three sequential activities: (1) "Name a time you felt bored." (2) "What did you do when you felt bored?" (3) "What else could you have done when you were bored?"

For a prompt that consists of more than one question, any student may stop after the first one. For example, they would name a time they were bored and stop there or explain what they did the last time they were bored but not offer other response options. If this happens, students (whether in need of special education support or not) may require follow-up prompting, saying, "So what did you do when you felt that way?" or "Did that strategy work? What could you do differently next time?" These are strategies that most teachers use instinctively and should be applied to MCCs, as well.

If you are working with self-contained classes, which have a smaller number of students and may support a range of classifications in your building, you should adapt MCCs for these students as well. (This applies whether you are the teacher or a school mental health professional visiting the classroom.) The smaller class size allows a unique chance to give more students a chance to speak and create a classroom community. If you teach a self-contained class with a 12:1:2 or 15:1:1 ratio of special education students to staff members, it is likely that your students have at least some verbal, academic, and social skills, along with academic and/or behavioral management needs that interfere with their ability to learn in a general education setting.

Similar to the aforementioned inclusion model, consider how a prompt might be adapted within this type of self-contained classroom. Consider the same prompt: "When do you feel bored? What are all the ways you have dealt with being bored? What other ideas might work?" Differing from the inclusion class, a special education teacher in this situation may decide to paraphrase the prompt when first presenting it. Similarly, the teacher might consider writing it down on the board, showing it on a screen, or printing it on the desk for some or all students. Make no assumptions about vocabulary—nothing is lost by reviewing. For example, the key word here is "bored," so you may want to ask students, "What does the word 'bored' mean?" Doing this with any questionable words should be a standard practice for MCCs in self-contained settings.

Again, as this example has multiple questions, it would be advisable to break the question into more manageable parts. For instance, the Conversation Leader might start with "Name a time you have felt bored." After the students have had a chance to answer that, the teacher might then ask, "What do you typically do to stop feeling bored?" If the student shares, "I usually look at my phone," as a response, the Conversation Leader can ask the follow-up question, "What else could you do to help yourself?" in the moment rather than giving multiple questions to start. The student's response might be followed by "What do others do when they are bored?" and then "What is a question you want to ask one of your groupmates about what they just said?" The latter query is designed to help promote cross-student conversation and is a good one to remember for all MCC contexts.

Another helpful tool for students, both special education and otherwise, would be to provide personal examples. For instance, a Conversation Leader might say, "I feel most bored when I am waiting in line at the grocery store. Can you think of a time when you felt bored?" By providing a sample response, students are given clarity in the expectation. For students who might still struggle to answer an open-ended question, it may be helpful to use a sentence starter for support. For instance, the Conversation Leader might say, "Finish this sentence 'I feel bored when ...'" These are just a few of the ways to accommodate the varying needs within a self-contained class. It is left up to the expertise of special education teachers to determine which adaptations would be appropriate for each student.

Some of the MCC prompts require communication that might make them challenging for students in self-contained classes that solely target life skills/adaptive functioning, applied behavior analysis, or classes with students who have very limited verbal communication (e.g., 8:1:1 and 6:1:1). This likely will require alteration in the goal of these prompts to target more appropriate areas, such as eye contact, taking turns, and hearing what someone else said.

Using the same prompt about boredom as an example, the introduction might include the usage of pictures, a "repeat after me" structure and/or forced choice. As students within this class may not understand the teacher's verbal explanation, a simple picture of someone looking bored could cue the student into the conversation. After cuing students in, the teacher might have the students repeat, "When I feel bored I ..." to see if the student could answer the question. To promote conversational skills, a Conversation Leader might say, "Ask Tommy what he does when he feels bored," and similarly help structure each students' response, thereby creating a kind of "conversation." For those with limited verbal capacity, a series of pictures may be provided and the student would be asked to point to what they do when they are bored. While this prompt is presented in a more basic format, there are still ways to build essential skills to facilitate group conversation and target social-emotional goals.

Although the sample prompts provided in Appendices A through C of this book may be challenging for students within this type of class, the MCC structure allows for creation of suitable prompts. Chapter 3 reviews the process for selecting MCC prompts, and it is suggested that a special educator use this structure to formulate questions that are more appropriate for a population with limited verbal communication skills.

HOW DO YOU INCLUDE ELLS IN MCCS?

As noted earlier, MCCs should be treated similarly to any other lesson within the classroom. If you are a teacher with a few ELLs in your class, how would you typically include them in other discussion-based lessons? ELLs often are supported by a professional, generally referred to as an English as a New Language (ENL) or an English as a Second Language (ESL) teacher, who has a specific certification in how to best accommodate these students. Use this teacher as a resource in how to most effectively engage all learners!

Similar to the other variations of student differences, ELLs span a wide range of language acquisition phases. Depending on the stage of language acquisition, involvement in MCCs may look different. For instance, you might make a regular practice of defining vocabulary words that are part of the prompts and keeping a word wall list. Making vocabulary identification a regular practice creates less stigma for students with limited vocabularies regardless of the reason. Future prompts can be built from those vocabulary words.

As another consideration, a student who may be in the "silent period" will be less involved in this activity compared to an ELL that attains basic interpersonal communicative skills (BICS). Regardless of the stage of development, both students are learning from the experience of MCC and the main goal is always to make all ELLs feel like part of the classroom community, both during MCCs and beyond. Regardless of students' language status, the skills and virtues that MCCs promote are essential for their well-being. Therefore, it is suggested that students are met where they are and not expected to participate in a way that would be uncomfortable for them but that you do find ways to elicit their participation.

Consider the same sample MCC that has been used throughout this chapter through the lens of potential levels of language acquisition for ELLs. When presenting to a student who takes in the new language but cannot speak it, the student should not be expected to participate verbally to any significant degree. It may be beneficial to ask the student(s) in this phase to provide a nonverbal cue if they agree or disagree with something shared about boredom or draw a picture of what they do when they are bored so all students are able to stay engaged.

For those students who can interpret the new language and speak in short phrases, and potentially even sentences, there may be a level of anxiety that comes with speaking in front of peers and/or staff members with which they are unfamiliar. They can share their answer with a trusted staff member, or perhaps a language buddy, to practice and build confidence and then hopefully share an utterance with the class. Additionally, to facilitate their creativity, providing a sentence structure such as "Instead of ____ when I am bored, I could ____" and/or use a visual to ignite their production of language. Students beyond this level of language acquisition are proficient and expected to participate in verbal discussions within the classroom. As this exploration demonstrates, each student has a unique set of needs; therefore, it is up to the Conversation Leader's discretion to use any scaffolding that seems appropriate.

Additionally, a common practice of ENL teachers is pre-teaching some of the classroom content either the day before or prior to the class. Individuals are more comfortable when they know what is expected. Similarly, many ELLs increase their engagement if they have prior exposure to a topic. If you are collaborating with an ENL teacher, it is recommended that you share the prompts in advance and allow them to use their expertise to determine if a student needs prior exposure to and preparation for that MCC. Additionally, the ENL teacher and the Conversation Leader can work together to determine appropriate times for ELLs' participation and to prepare students appropriately for increased comfort. Through a combination of tailoring prompts and preparing ELLs, these students will feel part of the classroom community and worthy of participating in the future. The key point is the need to facilitate genuine conversations among all children to the extent possible, in appropriate modalities, as this is an essential life skill that will benefit them to whatever extent they possess it.

WHAT ADAPTATIONS ARE RECOMMENDED IF YOU WORK WITH GIFTED STUDENTS?

Differentiation in a setting with gifted students requires accommodating to ensure appropriate challenge and engagement. Some of the sample prompts may seem too elementary to especially bright students in your class. Feel free to expand on prompts and allow for creativity, regardless of the level of your students.

When working with the gifted population, it is important to get student buy-in and allow space for choice. Students within this population may resist because they are uncomfortable in the unstructured, interpersonal context that MCCs represent. Just as you would connect academic content to life outcomes, it is suggested that Conversation Leaders explicitly teach students the connection between social-emotional learning (SEL) skills and success in careers. For instance, a Conversation Leader may say, "Collaboration and emotion recognition are skills you may be asked about in a future interview. Do you know how you have acquired these skills? What other social and emotional skills might you need in order to be successful in your career?"

Consistent with the preceding, a general strategy with this subgroup is to give them more latitude in framing the exact way the prompt is designed. Each day, the next day's prompt can be presented in its current form along with this question: "Here is what our MCC will be about tomorrow. How would you like to modify or expand this to make for a better discussion?" This can be done as a whole class and/or by designating individuals or pairs of students to work on this on a rotating basis. Of course, these activities themselves promote conversation and students' use and development of SEL skills!

Additional guidance comes from continuing with the example of the prompt on boredom. Gifted students often find it helpful to work from a concrete example. You might first generate a list of situations in which students might feel bored. Then, prompts can be drawn from those particulars. A Conversation Leader might say something like, "When you feel a teacher is moving too slow on a subject you already understand, share some ways you can address this so that you don't lose interest in that class or that lesson." Then, you might say, "Have a discussion on what else you might do in those situations." This brings into play another tool, recommended throughout other chapters, which is to utilize group work during MCCs. It may be fruitful to break off into groups, which will allow gifted students to get more practice in working together and challenging themselves in unexpected ways.

WILL CULTURALLY DIVERSE CLASSROOMS RAISE CONFLICT DURING MCCS?

Now, more than ever, conversations about race and culture are at the forefront of our American society. After George Floyd was killed in May 2020, nationwide protests occurred and continue to occur as of this writing, bringing further light to racial inequality in society. The 2021 storming of the US Capitol was a demonstration of rioting and violence, continuing to highlight the polarization of our political parties and government officials. Schieble et al. (2020) eloquently highlight the inequities in social, political, and economic policies and the need for having conversations about them in the classroom, despite the fear of challenges that may arise. The authors state, "Critical conversations matter in schools because they tackle the very real, systemic inequities that exist in our society. If we are to foster discussions about *How should we live together?*, these discussions must embed the reality that we presently live together in highly inequitable ways that are neither by accident or natural order, but by social design" (Schieble et al., 2020, p. 3).

It is inevitable for some of the MCCs to address topics such as culture, race, gender, and identity, so leave room for variations in responses among your students. MCCs are meant to be a broader conversation that sets the foundation for the development of a student's positive purpose, including a desire for social change. Indeed, the question prompts often are designed to tap into students' own experiences and preferences in order to promote sharing. Adolescents often have, and should learn how to express, strong opinions and respond to those of others in civil and respectful ways while still feeling empowered to disagree.

Because students' experiences can vary considerably, cultural sensitivity and humility are required when starting any conversation in class. For example, as a general observation, in individualistic cultures, developing autonomy and self-reliance is emphasized, while in collectivist cultures, individuals tend to prioritize the group over the self. How might this relate to MCCs? Think about how the responses to a question about a role model might differ for a Japanese student who recently immigrated to the United States and a student who was born and raised in New York City. Yet, consider also that Conversation Leaders often will not know the detailed cultural and ethnic background of individual students. Many socialization influences affect a given student's perspective on role models, with far more nuance and variation than you would want to infer based on a broad knowledge of race or culture. The most important thing to do is to allow students to feel heard and understood and to educate you about their cultural frame of reference, hence the need for cultural humility. Correspondingly, because you cannot predict where all conversations will go, reinforcing and referring to the *brave space* concept is especially relevant because inadvertent cultural "mistakes" inevitably will be made. You do not want such instances to stifle conversation and disclosure. Indeed, through your modeling, you will help students understand how to handle difficult conversations.

The "unexpected" response can lead Conversation Leaders and other school personnel to create assignments or other opportunities that will allow students to share their cultural identities. This can avert stereotyping, increase student comfort, and provide new ideas for MCC prompts. There is no "right" answer for a question about a student's role model; instead, Conversation Leaders should consider how to embrace the uniqueness of each individual response. Allowing for individuality and different cultural backgrounds to actively become a part of MCCs, without creating conflict, is an ultimate aspiration.

As mentioned in Chapter 3, rules and norms will help to keep students on track with expectations. Therefore, when establishing the ground rules for MCCs, be sure to bring up the considerations that occur or will occur with regularity so that the group can anticipate what is expected/unexpected. If it was not brought up during the establishing of norms, don't hesitate to revisit the list to add items related to how to respect differences while communicating.

HOW CAN PERSONALITY STYLES IMPACT MCCS?

Personality is an interesting topic when considering group discussions, such as MCCs. For instance, it is typical for a classroom to have both students who are extremely extroverted as well as students who are particularly introverted. As educators learn quickly, not all students will feel comfortable being vulnerable in front of the class. While this may seem daunting when opening up the floor for discussion, think about how you manage differing comfort levels during other times. It is highly likely that you have had group discussions prior to your new MCCs, so what do you typically do in order to balance the different personalities in the group? These ideas can be adapted to apply to MCCs.

One way to support the comfort of sharing is to model vulnerability. While it is absolutely necessary to foster a contributory classroom climate, it is also okay to show the students that you are human and answer the MCC prompt yourself before opening up the floor. In fact, students benefit from knowing that you are not perfect! If you are asking kids to talk about feelings such as sadness, anger, and confusion, Conversation Leaders need to be willing to do the same. By your modeling vulnerability, the students are more likely to risk being vulnerable too. Students resonate particularly strongly to stories about how you—who they respect and to whom they often invest supreme powers—came to start to manage your strong emotions (still without complete success) when you were their age. Middle schoolers, in particular, need help taking a more realistic look at others they tend to stereotype or whose attributes they exaggerate. Fostering openness in the classroom by both educators and students also allows for a stronger classroom community and more positive student–teacher and student–student relationships.

Students also vary in how comfortable they feel communicating with peers or with adult authority figures, that is, teachers, school mental health professionals, and administrators, in an unstructured conversation context. While this may seem like a given, it is common for many students to talk directly to the Conversation Leader during a conversation and await a response, but it is recommended that Conversation Leaders redirect questions and comments back to the group. The MCCs are not meant to be a lecture or individual student dialogues with the Conversation Leader but rather a collaborative process where all participants are treated as equals. When there is a format that encourages equality across group participants, Conversation Leader(s) included, students are more likely to feel comfortable and safe to share their opinions. Remember, the vast majority of prompts take the form of opinion questions, and the opinions of the Conversation Leader are just that—opinions, not facts to be learned. One way to keep the group in focus is to introduce the prompt and have students discuss in pairs and trios before sharing out with the larger group. Teachers can determine who does the sharing out, keeping track to make sure that everyone gets a turn. This format can be interspersed as needed with the usual prompt going out to the whole group.

As mentioned in Chapter 5, teachers in the pilot work also found it helpful to leave alternative ways for students to share their thoughts. If a Conversation Leader is working on a virtual platform, this may be a more effective way to engage all students. As it is hard to avoid talking over others in a Google Meet or Zoom meeting, it may be more effective to facilitate a conversation using the chat features or other options. For instance, Conversation Leaders can create a Google form or an anonymous posting capacity that allows for commenting.

As this chapter comes to a close, if you are saying, "I still need help with appropriately modifying my MCCs for my class," your suggested next step is to collaborate with colleagues. If there is a special education teacher, ENL teacher, or other school professional that may be well equipped to support your needs, feel free to reach out to them. Additionally, school psychologists (immodestly speaking!) are a great resource for differentiation, modification, and accommodations.

Chapter Wrap-Up

We provided guidelines and examples for how to differentiate the MCC structure for the unique needs of your students. We discussed the importance of respect and inclusiveness when considering students' wide range of cognitive abilities, personalities, and cultural backgrounds. Throughout, we emphasized that many of the ways in which you have already modified other group discussions to tailor to diverse student needs will be applicable to MCCs as well. If you find a student having continued frustration and difficulty, or otherwise unsatisfied with MCCs in meeting their needs, we mentioned school psychologists and counselors as helpful resources, as their training has made them well equipped to support your journey through individualizing your MCCs. Remember that, in order to create an inclusive classroom environment, modifying and accommodating is a continuous process!

Reflective Conversations for Growth

Now that you have learned about the basic strategies for individualizing MCCs and creating an inclusive MCC environment to meet all of your students' needs, reflect on/ write down the following and commit to taking the appropriate follow-up actions in order to continue to learn and grow as a Conversation Leader.

ACTION STEPS/PRIORITIES

In order to be an effective Conversation Leader, it will be important to reflect on your own diversity. What makes you unique? What experiences of your students are most unfamiliar to you? How might this impact your MCCs?

Are there any colleagues that can help you prepare for differentiation? For instance, if you have any ELLs, who is the ENL/ESL teacher who might be able to ensure you are effectively engaging these students?

_____

_____

_____

ADAPTATIONS

What are some of the areas of diversity among your students? Which part of this chapter will help you most when preparing to individualize your MCCs (recognizing that this chapter is not an exhaustive list of the possible diversities in a group)?

_____

_____

_____

CHALLENGES

Topics about race, gender, and ethnicity may lead to debate or discomfort within your classroom. How will you encourage respectful debate, students "living with discomfort," and constructively resolve conflict?

_____

_____

_____

QUESTIONS

What questions still remain after reading Chapter 7? Who might be well equipped to support you? For instance, school psychologists, ENL teachers, counselors, and social workers are well positioned to support in effectively engaging diverse learners.

_____

_____

_____

CHAPTER 8

Three-Year Developmental Progression

C hapter 2 provided you with in-depth information about the Morning Classroom Conversation (MCC) structure, and Chapters 3 and 6 assisted you with finding the implementation style that works best for your group, so now it is time to take a deeper look at one of the most important MCC dimensions: the three-year developmental progression. As noted earlier, this progression is a key step in allowing students to fully internalize these skills and make it a part of who they are and how they handle the world around them. In this chapter, the importance of the three-year progression is discussed, along with several sample progressions in various months to see how a prompt can evolve over time to match the development of the child and their skill level. Finally, a sample alternative implementation style specific to the three-year progression is provided and discussed.

 WHAT IS THE THREE-YEAR DEVELOPMENTAL SEQUENCE?

The unique progression of a three-year structure allows students the opportunity to reflect on similar MCCs and revisit familiar concepts, which creates a deeper level of understanding over time. In Year 1, the conversation topics ask students to self-reflect for a better understanding of themselves and their own skills and virtues; in Year 2, they are asked to think about their school; finally, in Year 3, they are prompted to widen their focus beyond the school building into their larger community and the world. In Chapter 2, the MCC yearly progression was discussed as one of the four dimensions of MCCs. Provided in the following is a detailed look at what this progression looks like in practice, as well as sample questions for each month to illustrate the "MCC yearly progression."

Each yearly progression presented in the MCC format is created with adolescent development in mind, recognizing that students' capacities for widening their cognitive and social awareness lenses increase from year to year. Let's start by looking at the first year of MCC prompts, known as *Better Me*. These prompts focus on providing questions that promote self-improvement, self-reflection, self-awareness, and intrinsic motivation to develop a positive purpose on an individual level. The rationale is that students must first get to know themselves—their skills, virtues, and perspectives with relation to their own growth. Of course, this is not "new" for students, but they rarely have been guided to probe these areas of their lives intentionally and in an ongoing way. The goal here is to broaden and more deeply elaborate their self-schema (McArthur et al., 2019). Adolescents can then begin to understand what they can improve upon with regard to their fundamental social-emotional learning (SEL) skills and virtues before taking these competencies and expanding the impact they can have on their environment.

The *Better School* prompts, which are next in the MCC developmental progression, encourage students to build upon their skill set from the previous year as well as their growing cognitive and emotional development, with a goal of expanding their thoughts to their immediate communities. This focus could include their local neighborhood, their school as a whole, or their classroom/group community. The goal for a *Better School* mindset is to provide students with questions that challenge their level of thinking and self-reflection and extend their positive purpose beyond their own well-being. Students are guided to consider that although self-improvement and self-reflection are invaluable to their own growth, using their skills to improve the lives of those around them will help to improve their overall environment and will thus be a win–win for everyone, including themselves.

The last level of focus in the MCC yearly progression is the *Better World* prompts, which are designed to further challenge students to expand positive purpose to include their own place in the world. The goal of these prompts is to assist students with expanding their worldview beyond themselves and their immediate community to also include the larger communities of which they are a part. This can include reflection and improvement upon the community, state, country in which they reside, or the world, overall. For some students, this is the most eye-opening stage. Many students don't see themselves as effective active agents in the world. They don't see themselves as having the potential for wider influence, and they don't have in their regular awareness the interconnections they have with so many others.

 ## WHAT IF YOU ONLY HAVE YOUR STUDENTS FOR ONE YEAR?

For those who may be concerned about their group of students having exposure to only one year of MCCs, you may be wondering do students need three years of MCC exposure to be successful in achieving beneficial SEL growth? In short, no. Although the MCC yearly progression is the ideal scenario for students, it is understood that, similar to the weekly and monthly schedules, the ideal is not always possible. Investigating whether this progression is feasible is a primary determinant. Indeed, on one hand, learning concepts progressively over time is the preferred scenario for all new topics presented to students. However, on the other hand, given that the MCC yearly progression does weigh heavily on the natural developmental level of students, in theory, each year can be given in solitude with the same level of success. So, the inevitable follow-up questions must be addressed: If you only anticipate your students to have one year of exposure to MCC, which year do you choose?

The factors to focus on when answering this question for your specific group of students are where they are, developmentally, their ability level, any external factors that may be impacting them in the classroom, and any specific area that your class as a whole would benefit from focusing on. There also may be situations where your students have been exposed to social-emotional and character development interventions in their recent past, which may make them a better candidate for Year 2 or Year 3 than if they had no exposure to these areas. But this is not typical; more likely is that your class will have wide variation in students' prior exposure to SEL. And even those students may not have been exposed to character development concepts of virtues (or, if they have been exposed to character virtues, they may not have been exposed to SEL). Hence, each of these progressions complements one another and builds in a way that helps students better understand themselves and the world around them in a supportive and approachable context.

SAMPLE THREE-YEAR MORNING CLASSROOM CONVERSATIONS SEQUENCE

Provided next are additional examples using explicit MCC prompts for a few select months to showcase how the prompts evolve over each year. Within each sample below, there is one prompt provided for Year 1, Year 2, and Year 3 that coincide with each other in the MCC yearly progression. As you review each month, you will notice that the overall concepts are parallel but altered slightly to align with the *Better Me–Better School–Better World* developmental focus. These samples help you as a Conversation Leader to visualize how the prompts progress and become more broadening and challenging from year to year.

November/Month One: Making Ourselves, School, and World Better

- Year 1 (*Better Me*): Name at least one reason why you feel safe at school.
- Year 2 (*Better School*): It is so important for school to be a safe place for students, teachers, and administrators. How do you think this school can be made an even safer place?
- Year 3 (*Better World*): What place do you consider the safest place in the world? Why?

For this example, the Year 1 prompt asks students to think about and potentially verbalize components of their environment that help them feel safe in school, which requires introspection and allows the students to learn about their needs within their immediate environment. The Year 2 prompt expands this topic of safety at school beyond themselves to consider those around them. Such a focus also helps students think about ways to improve their environment for the sake of others. Year 3 continues the developmental progression of the topics mentioned in Year 1 and 2 regarding safety by applying it to the student's larger environment and the world. Thinking about safety in this way allows students an opportunity to explore what makes the world feel safe or unsafe and how they individuals can have an impact on it.

February/Month Four: Showing Resilience and Overcoming Obstacles

- Year 1 (*Better Me*): Think of one person you admire. Do they believe they can get through hard times? How do you know?
- Year 2 (*Better School*): Name one difficult experience that you experienced this year at school. What did you learn from overcoming this obstacle?
- Year 3 (*Better World*): Thinking about racism, do you think it is possible to fully forget about a problem that occurred in your past? If yes, how? If no, how does this memory impact you?

The earlier Year 1 prompt has a *Better Me* focus by prompting students to think about qualities that they personally find admirable in others and how these traits may foster resilience. This would ideally help them think about how to apply these attributes to their own life. With the Year 2 prompt, students are asked to reflect on how they overcame difficult experiences at school, expanding to the *Better School* target. The *Better World* prompt advances these thoughts on overcoming difficult situations to apply to racism, a more challenging and thought-provoking topic. This helps students apply resilience to larger communities, as racism is a systemic and worldwide issue.

April/Month Six: Connecting With Others and Being a Leader

- Year 1 (*Better Me*): How has leadership been defined in your life? Who has taught you to be a leader?
- Year 2 (*Better School*): How is this school helping you develop yourself as a leader? Are there any barriers to leadership in our school building?
- Year 3 (*Better World*): How does leadership impact your ability to succeed in the world? How are all successful people leaders?

In these prompts, the topic is leadership. Year 1 discusses leadership as it pertains to students' own lives, their personal actions and experiences. Year 2 asks students to reflect further on how their leadership skills have developed not just through their own experiences but through their interactions with others. This prompt allows students to consider how leading others can sometimes be difficult within a school. Furthermore, Year 3 encourages students to see their leadership abilities through the lens of global impact and general success in life. The revisiting of this topic and others over multiple years makes large scale topics, such as global impact and leadership, more approachable for students to explore.

What should now become clear after you've familiarized yourself with some sample MCC yearly progressions is that there is an immense amount of growth that can come from revisiting previous topics from a more experienced and advanced lens. Even though students may not remember topics discussed in previous years, they can still utilize the SEL skills gained earlier in the year and in previous years to sufficiently respond to more advanced topics. You will see this from how they build on skill benefits that were gained from MCCs in the past, along with their natural growth and development, to think about and respond to new prompts in increasingly nuanced and sophisticated ways.

SAMPLE ADAPTED THREE-YEAR SEQUENCE FOR ONE YEAR OF IMPLEMENTATION

Thanks to the variety of samples provided in Chapter 6, you should feel confident that there will be an MCC style to fit your group, whether it be a traditional MCC group or otherwise. Since there are inevitably going to be MCC groups that, for whatever reason, may not be able to have three years of exposure to MCCs, this section shows how all three progression levels can be targeted. Table 8.1 considers an 18-week structure with a target on Empathy. The first six weeks of this group target self-development, Weeks 7 through 12 allow students to expand to thinking about others within the school and Weeks 13 through 18 further explore empathy throughout the wider world.

As you will notice over the 18 sessions, this group follows the trajectory of *Better Me–Better School–Better World*, in a format that allows all progressions to be discussed within one school year. Doing so allows for increased sophistication in conversation as the year progresses, if an 18-session structure is possible. However, you might also consider focusing only on *Better Me* prompts throughout all 18 weeks, if you feel your group requires more basic personal skill building before moving on to applying the skill in a school and community context. Keep in mind that this sample, similar to others discussed in Chapter 6, can be altered to fit your needs and your circumstances.

TABLE 8.1 ● Skill: Empathy

BETTER ME	
Session 1	What is empathy? How do you feel when someone else shows empathy toward you? How do you know when someone is showing you empathy?
Session 2	A new student just arrived at your school. What do you think it feels like to be living in a new place with all new people? Has this happened to you?
Session 3	In many situations, it's important for others to know we are paying attention to them. How can you nonverbally demonstrate that you are actively listening to your peers?

BETTER ME	
Session 4	Why does it usually feel good to share our feelings with others, whether positive or negative?
Session 5	Why might people not listen to new ideas? What helps you to be more likely to listen to new or different ideas?
Session 6	"Don't judge others unless you are standing in their shoes." Do you agree with that quote? What does it have to do with empathy?

BETTER SCHOOL	
Session 7	What do you think it feels like to be a principal? What is the hardest part of their job?
Session 8	Why is it important to keep an open mind about others' differences? What would happen if we were close-minded at this school?
Session 9	Where in school do we have the opportunity to share our feelings? How could we create more of these spaces?
Session 10	In school, it can be difficult to control our impulses or desires to call out. For some, it is easier than for others. What could we do to help decrease the amount of times a day that people talk over each other?
Session 11	If administrators had more open forums to hear how students felt about different issues, would it make the school better? Why or why not?
Session 12	At school, how do some of your teachers show you empathy? What makes you feel most understood and comfortable in the classroom?

BETTER WORLD	
Session 13	There are many people who did not have enough money to afford dinner last night. How do you think they feel?
Session 14	Do you have to accept and love all ideas in order to be a loyal member of the United States?
Session 15	Does our social media–filled world create too much emotional sharing? Why or why not?
Session 16	If politicians had more open forums to hear the perspective of local individuals, do you think this would make things better or worse? Why?
Session 17	What are some ways that our country can improve in the next five years? How will demonstrating empathy impact the success of our country?
Session 18	Do local leaders need to show empathy? Why or why not?

Chapter Wrap-Up

To further illustrate "the big picture" of MCCs, we provided samples of the three-year progression (*Better Me–Better School–Better World*) as well as a sample alternative version of implementing all three progressions over one year. Year 1 in the progression focuses on self-improvement and awareness, Year 2 on helping those in their immediate surrounding community, and Year 3 on creating positive impacts on larger communities and the world. The sample progressions provided help depict how each year expands and challenges students' thinking while providing continuity with prior prompts and underlying skills, virtues, and themes. Following this progression, whether it be in the traditional format over three years, or alternatively over one year, maximizes the potential of students' social and emotional growth upon concluding MCCs after Year 3.

 Reflective Conversations for Growth

Now that you have been able to see samples of the MCC yearly progression, reflect on/write down the following and commit to taking the appropriate follow-up actions in order to continue to learn and grow as a Conversation Leader.

ACTION STEPS/PRIORITIES

What "Year" will your students be in this year for their MCC sequence? What is most important within this year for your students to focus on that aligns best with their needs? (For example, if your students will begin this year using Year 2, they may benefit most from focusing on their classroom community, their school community, their teachers/support staff/administrators, etc.)

_____

_____

_____

What adaptations might you make to how you present and conduct MCCs based on whether students have had MCCs before or based on whatever social-emotional and character development efforts might be under way in your classroom/school/setting?

_____

_____

_____

CHALLENGES

How will you adapt to scheduling irregularities, for example, due to weather days, other unanticipated disruptions in a weekly schedule, to ensure that your students get as much well-rounded exposure to MCCs as possible?

_____

_____

_____

QUESTIONS

What questions still remain after reading Chapter 8? Consider submitting one or two questions to the authors at MorningClassroomConversations@gmail.com.

_____

_____

_____

CHAPTER 9

Implementation Considerations for Lead Teachers and/or Administrators

Most of this book has targeted the audience of a Conversation Leader or the individual who would be directly facilitating Morning Classroom Conversations (MCCs) with students. In an effort to target more school personnel, this chapter targets a new audience: lead teachers, administrators, and/or other staff who are involved with schoolwide or districtwide systems needed to set the foundation of MCCs and support coordinated implementation. At its best, MCCs are a three-year process for students. This means that ideally, there would be a system that would allow for coordinating MCCs across classrooms and grade levels over time, which would allow a given group of students to experience the full three-year developmental sequence. This chapter is directed at the action steps necessary for making effective system-level change, in order to best support MCC implementation.

THE CORE TEAM

Picture a principal, school counselor, various teachers (Math, Social Studies, English, Physical Education, etc.), club advisors, and a psychologist discussing MCCs—meeting to brainstorm, monitor MCC effectiveness, and problem solve. In schools that piloted MCCs, this team of people was called a "Core Team" and was created to improve communication and coordination around MCCs across classrooms and over time. Regardless of the name you choose for this committee or if your district has a social-emotional consultant to support it, a multidisciplinary team is a useful way to launch MCCs within your school and will be especially useful in expanding and monitoring success once MCCs are launched in a few classrooms.

A key function of a Core Team is to guide and monitor the implementation of MCCs in a way that supports the three-year developmental sequence. This requires collaboration and coordination of staff within and across grade levels. It also requires the capacity to troubleshoot and problem solve as the inevitable obstacles arise. Fortunately, pilot work with MCCs and other social-emotional learning (SEL) interventions provide insight into the nature of these issues and allow Core Teams to design proactive processes to minimize disruption and get things back on track in the event that things run off the rails a bit. Here are some questions to guide Core Team organization and functioning, followed by an elaboration of best practice considerations for each area:

1. How engaged are the students in MCCs? For which students does it seem to be going well? Less well? How do we know? Are there ways to make MCCs more engaging? As discussed in Chapters 1 and 5, it might be helpful to review the responses from the student or teacher rubrics within Appendix D.

2. From the staff perspective, what is currently going well with MCCs? How can more of this be done?

3. What barriers do Conversation Leaders mention? How is the allotted 10- to 15-minute time frame working? How can the Core Team help?

By asking targeted questions about the effectiveness of the program, the team can work together to problem solve. Of course, when implementation of MCC in a school is systematic, the information the Core Team gathers across MCC implementers shapes evaluation and feedback to individual Conversation Leaders.

ASSESSING ENGAGEMENT AND IMPACT

Engagement is a necessary condition for the success of MCCs or any SEL-related activity. If staff or students don't find MCCs engaging, the resulting learning will be minimized. For example, one Core Team in a pilot school discussed that students were not "tuned in to the MCC channel," leaving little opportunity to have productive MCCs and create a community. The Core Team was encouraged to visit MCCs in different classes to assess what was happening and discuss specific ways to try engaging students in the future. In this instance, there was a single Conversation Leader mentioning his challenge within his seventh-grade English classes, so the Core Team suggested strategies this particular teacher could try within his group. If the engagement issue was more widespread, the leader of the Core Team could discuss the engagement techniques during an upcoming faculty meeting or department meeting(s).

The rubrics that are offered within this book to be completed by Conversation Leaders (as well as students; see Appendix D) also speak to the extent of student engagement. Much as individual Conversation Leaders review their own rubrics, and those of students, the Core Team takes a look at all of the data from the MCC rubrics to get a complete picture of how effective the MCCs seem to be within and across grade levels. Are there grade levels where MCCs seem to be going particularly well or poorly? Do some subgroups of students (or staff) seem to find MCCs more or less engaging and effective? The Core Team tries to grasp the big picture and follow up in a supportive, encouraging, and constructive way.

HIGHLIGHTING "SMALL WINS"

Core Teams can become solely problem-focused and forget to recognize MCC successes. A key function of effective Core

Teams is to highlight "small wins" or moments of success within MCCs. For this to happen systematically, Core Teams will need a process to gather information about what is working for the Conversation Leaders and the students, review it, and share best practices. Through this sharing, other Conversation Leaders will have an opportunity to learn from their colleagues and bring those ideas into their own MCCs. Sharing and celebrating what is going right is just as constructive as correcting what needs improvements!

Let's consider a more specific example. Mrs. Santiago, a school counselor, regularly asks seventh-grade MCC Conversation Leaders that she checks in with and supports to let her know about successes. During her Core Team meeting, she shares what she learned from Mr. Arias, who runs MCCs at the start of his English language arts (ELA) class: "I have been starting my class off with a song each day, as the students transition into my room. They know once the song is complete, it is time for the MCC. Sometimes, I let students pick the song we will use later in the week—there have been times they need to introduce me to an artist because all of the kids know the song, but I don't!" The assistant principal, who chairs the Core Team, has a weekly email to her staff that includes a calendar with upcoming events, building news, and peer strategies for effective teaching. The assistant principal shares this tip in a section of her weekly email called "Effectively Connecting with Our Students." Mr. Arias smiles because he knows why Conversation Leaders in the teachers' lounge are talking about the music they use to introduce their MCCs.

NAVIGATING INSTRUCTIONAL BARRIERS

Every instructional innovation—and that's what MCCs are when they get introduced—runs into some kind of barrier at one point or another. Core Teams must follow their regular requests for updates about successes to include challenges or barriers that Conversation Leaders face. When Core Teams open up the floor to sharing difficulties, the Conversation Leaders feel like their voices can be heard and they are not expected to overcome all challenges on their own.

If the Core Team targets specific questions (e.g., "How is the allotted 10- to 15-minute time frame working?" "How is the transition from the MCC to the next subject area?" "How are you managing with homeroom tasks and getting MCCs done well?"), there is a goal in mind which allows the Team to stay on task and utilize time wisely. It is likely that Core Team meetings will need to be before/after school or during planning time (typically 40–45 minutes and no less than monthly), so a targeted conversation may help in using time as effectively as possible. Whether the conversation is broad or targeted, the problem-solving model should be intentional. The Core Team can identify problems, review possible solutions with consequences, come up with the best option together, and determine who will speak with the Conversation Leader(s) involved to follow up. Some common barriers that Conversation Leaders may encounter that can be addressed by the Core Team are the following:

- Particular students for whom MCCs do not seem to be working, whether general or special education
- Groups of students with various backgrounds and ability levels who tend to see themselves less well-represented in the prompts
- Impact of "breakfast before the bell" and morning announcements
- Disruptions in MCC flow because of disruptions in the usual schedule (e.g., for Instructional Rounds or other visits, weather-related lost time)
- Particular colleagues who do not seem to be implementing MCCs at all, or not regularly and in a rote manner

It is not unknown for staff who do not believe in the effectiveness of an intervention, or who are having difficulty or are uncomfortable carrying it out, to simply not do it (or do it in the most cursory manner). This happens with many programs and MCCs are no exception. The Core Team's ability to address this, and really any concerns, depends on their authority and credibility. When they fall under the responsibility of an effective school administrator, the staff comes to know that there is accountability for doing MCCs well because it provides life skills that all students need. It also helps when those selected to the Core Team have credibility as instructors and are respected as advocates for students and staff. This communicates that the point of getting feedback about MCCs is the spirit of improvement, not the joy of "Gotcha!" We have seen the damage done by Core Teams composed of people who just happen to not have other committee assignments or whose presence on other school committees was unwelcomed. In these cases, MCCs are much more likely to thrive without having a Core Team.

Ultimately, the Core Team must have the capacity to gather information systematically, particularly any "bad news." Some processes must be in place for regular sharing by Conversation Leaders of how things are going in the MCCs, and this process must have integrity; that is, it must be trusted. Of course, realistically, those of you who have been in schools long enough know that not everyone will disclose their difficulties or dislikes of the program. Yet, you have likely seen that the students eventually share the truth. Staff know this as well, and that is why capturing student voice is so vital. When a Core Team member asks a student how their discussion went yesterday during MCC and the student looks back with a blank stare (and was not absent), that becomes an indication that implementation might be a problem. Follow-up with classmates usually confirms the situation. Failure to follow through professionally threatens the integrity of any instructional process because they are developmental—kids who miss lessons and activities have gaps that subsequently disadvantage them in future months and years of MCCs. This is why the Core Team must be able to take action directly, or, more typically, report to a school administrator who is clearly empowered to monitor and correct the instructional process.

 OBSTACLES TO CORE TEAM FUNCTIONING

Administrators, lead teachers, and all those involved in a leadership capacity have likely participated in a committee before. Similar to other committees with which you have been involved, there are potential barriers that may arise and it is important to consider how to address these concerns.

1. *"There is not a good time to meet."* Teachers, administrators, and all school staff are extremely busy. While a Core Team sounds great, there is a strong likelihood that schools will argue that there is not enough time. A first step in responding to this barrier is considering how other committees in your school function. Do teachers often get coverage to problem solve regarding programming? Are there professional development days that could involve MCC on the agenda? These types of questions are a great start when considering the formulation of a Core Team and committing to a regular schedule of meetings. One pilot school ran the meeting before school, and another had teachers create smaller "core teams" within their department meetings and bring the concerns to an MCC point person within the building.

2. *"Our committee doesn't get along."* Of course, there are advantages to working with a multidisciplinary team, but there also could be disadvantages to having a wide range of opinions. The concept of "too many cooks in the kitchen," or the committee having a different idea of what might be the best solution for a presented problem, may cause some tension within a group. Similar to how an MCC requires ground rules and effective communication, it may be helpful to determine some strategies to keep the team as a cohesive unit. Administrators have plenty of experience in navigating the range of personalities and opinions within a room, but the committee is meant to be collaborative rather than directly facilitated by an administrator, and therefore, it may be helpful for the committee to have a preparatory conversation about navigating disagreement. (It is also the case that some Core Teams decide to not have an administrator formally part of the team but instead serve as the Core Team

supervisor, to provide both accountability and a vehicle for follow up with Core Team peers, when needed.)

3. *"We never get anything accomplished during these meetings."* Going back to the conversation of time, no one wants to waste time. Each meeting must have an agenda with specific talking points for the meetings, and meetings must be followed up with notes that include action steps determined, who is responsible, and the appropriate time frame. This is how all serious—and effective—committees work. Core Team members can send questions or topics to one member who can draft the agenda and help guide the time management throughout the group discussion, in order to make it through all the questions. Another member can be the note-taker, who also can monitor the delineation of clear action plans, timelines, and responsibilities. These roles also can rotate periodically. Being planful and realistic about how feedback will be gathered from staff about MCC implementation and how it will be compiled and shared is a key recurring agenda item. Some Core Teams find that math and computer teachers are great resources in setting up surveys and gathering and analyzing data. Use your school's resources to the fullest!

4. *"This involves more than our Core Team can take on."* In a large building or where there is a lot of turnover in the Core Team, training becomes an important consideration. The MCCs have been designed to be implemented by any certified teacher, school mental health professional, or youth group leader. Pilot schools have demonstrated that teams of teachers and Core Teams benefit from learning together. Professional development can be organized in ways that your school or district typically does, under the leadership of the Core Team. For example, the Core Team might facilitate discussion around how to implement and/or adapt MCCs that take place as part of a Professional Learning Community or a series of after school

meetings. An increasing number of schools hold professional development training around books. In this instance, for MCCs, the Core Team can arrange for groups of teachers to get and read this book. Individual Core Team members can be conveners and group facilitators, or the Core Team can train a group of teachers to run the discussions. Dividing the book into two to four parts would work best.

5. *"They are not going to listen to what we tell them to do, anyways."* It's true that the Core Team does not have, and does not want, coercive power over Conversation Leaders. This is where self-determination theory comes in (Ryan & Deci, 2000). In brief, the theory suggests that employees are most effective and motivated when three things are present: a feeling of autonomy, competence, and relatedness. Conversation Leaders must feel they have autonomy, which can be fostered by allowing their voice to be heard in creating prompts, articulating concerns, or planning implementation rollout. Competence was, in part, addressed earlier. This is handled through additional professional development about MCCs and can be accomplished by Core Team members offering to observe MCCs and provide constructive and supportive feedback. The last area within the self-determination theory is relatedness, which is the need to have close relationships with others. This is accomplished through several of the suggestions already provided, which serve to increase the dialogue between Conversation Leaders, as well as with members of the Core Team. Involving Conversation Leaders in the Core Team's process of gathering, compiling, and interpreting feedback from implementers and students also builds strong feelings of relatedness.

The "Reflective Conversations for Growth" at the end of the chapter provides an opportunity for more exploration into additional barriers not discussed in this chapter and can be revisited in the future as needed.

EMBEDDING MCCS INTO THE CURRENT SECD STRUCTURES

Does your school feel like social-emotional character development (SECD) programs are fragmented and you are struggling to generalize these topics beyond the explicit lessons? Some of the top researchers in SEL and SECD have called this the "Jumbled Schoolhouse" or the idea that many programs can be functioning independently rather than under one "roof" of SECD (Elias et al., 2015). Sometimes, when MCCs are brought into schools as part of SEL efforts, they can feel to implementers like "one more thing." This never bodes well for implementation success.

With that in mind, the following question may come to mind: *Are there ways to embed these concepts beyond the homeroom, club or academic class in which the MCCs are occurring?* The short answer is "Absolutely!" The long answer is "The way to do that might look different, depending on the SECD already in place within your school."

At the time of this writing, restorative practices and anti-racism are two emerging emphases in our schools. Obviously, they cannot be addressed fully here. However, there are principles of MCCs that have great resonance with both of these areas. Restorative circles and practices in general are built upon trust, empathy, forgiveness, optimism, and the capacity for genuine exchange. The synergy with MCCs and this form of SECD is clear. In any school focusing on restorative practices or disciplinary systems with clear input from students, encouraging MCCs will strengthen those efforts.

Consider the value of using MCC prompts to stimulate respectful conversation between two students engaged in conflict and meeting as part of restorative practices. It has also been found that when a student is in a disciplinary context, such as a meeting with a school disciplinarian or newly arrived to in-school detention or suspension (or their better-named relatives), having the person in charge pose an MCC prompt at the outset is a bellwether for what is to follow. If a student is unwilling or unable to respond to the prompt, then it's clear that the student's anger (or shame) is still substantial and that further attempts at communication or "programming" at the moment will not go well. The student will need space and time to gain control over strong emotions and be willing and able to engage in some conversation. Additionally, many of the MCCs are related to topics that can be reviewed across the school day, so it would be helpful to plan for a more universal approach to embedding themes. For subject-specific examples, see Chapter 5.

Similarly, antiracism is built on empathy, communication, social problem-solving, and, indeed, the entire scope of SEL skills and virtues emphasized in MCCs. Again, the common denominator is respectful, civil conversation. One could take the position that without establishing MCCs, it would be hard to imagine genuine antiracism conversations and initiatives to have lasting success. Perhaps the most important point is that genuine human conversation is fundamental to organized life. No matter what issues emerge in a school—both those that are familiar and those that might come up unexpectedly, as the pandemic did—conversations will be part of the response. Thus, having MCCs as part of your classroom and school can be seen as fundamental to accomplish several preestablished, schoolwide goals.

When embedding MCCs into the SECD framework of your district, the overall strategy for Core Teams is to "unjumble the schoolhouse" and see where MCCs can fit most naturally with existing efforts. Perhaps it aligns well with the advisory period. Perhaps the communication skill-building is a natural fit with ELA, social studies, or health curriculum expectations. A growing number of schools already have daily periods designated for SEL, from 15 to 40 minutes. MCCs can provide a consistent, developmental structure for those 15-minute opportunities and can also be used to kick off longer, 40-minute meetings. If explicit SEL or SECD programming is not currently part of your school's model, the Core Team can consider exploring options for bringing such programming into your school; considerable guidance exists for doing so (e.g., Durlak et al., 2015; Elias & Arnold, 2009; Novick et al., 2002).

Chapter Wrap-Up

In some schools, MCCs will be carried out by individual teachers; in others, there will be more systematic implementation. For administrators and other school leaders reading this chapter, we discussed the need to intentionally guide and monitor MCC implementation. We cover setting up a multidisciplinary group of professionals to guide the MCC journey (a Core Team), which can assess engagement, celebrate small wins, and navigate barriers. With an understanding that there is possibility of obstacles on the Core Team, as with any committee, we guided you through some potential solutions to ensuring an effective and supportive Team. Finally, with a goal of "unjumbling the schoolhouse" we discussed the importance of integrating MCCs into your existing SEL or character education structure.

 Reflective Conversations for Growth

Now that you have a deeper understanding of the ways to support MCCs within a system-level lens and how to prepare Conversation Leaders for implementation, reflect on/write down the following and commit to taking the appropriate follow-up actions in order to continue to learn and grow as a Conversation Leader.

ACTION STEPS/PRIORITIES

There are many techniques for guiding and monitoring MCC implementation within this chapter. Which of the ideas will be your first target? What is your priority among your action steps?

_____

_____

_____

(Continued)

ADAPTATIONS

What would a Core Team look like within your system? Who do you think you might involve in your Core Team? Is there a group that already exists that might be appropriate for embedding MCCs into team discussions?

_____

_____

_____

CHALLENGES

What barriers do you foresee with implementing and monitoring MCCs? How can you prevent this from becoming a concern? Who can help?

_____

_____

_____

QUESTIONS

What professional development might you or your colleagues need to support your feeling more confident and comfortable with MCCs and SEL in general?

What questions still remain after reading Chapter 9? If you want to talk more about how to embed this within your current SECD structures, we encourage you to connect with experts through SEL4US and/or your state affiliate.

_____

_____

_____

Appendix A

Year 1 Daily Prompts

November/Month One (Year 1—*Better Me*): Making Ourselves, School, and World Better

	MONDAY	TUESDAY	WEDNESDAY	THURSDAY	FRIDAY
Week 1	What new places in the world would you like to travel? What do you want to learn by traveling? (Theme: Making Ourselves, School, and World Better)	What is the biggest problem you are facing right now? How can Constructive Creativity—which involves brainstorming as many ways to solve a problem or get something done as possible—help? (Virtue: Constructive Creativity)	Describe a time you learned to think about a problem in a new way (with Constructive Creativity). Did anyone help you think in a new way? (Skill: Social Problem-Solving)	Can you think of a time you were honest even though it was hard? Have you ever told a harmless lie just to spare someone else's feelings? Just about everyone has. Does that make you dishonest? (Skill: Communication)	Everyone benefits from having a passion in their lives. Think about people you know. What are some of their passions? What are yours? (Theme: Making Ourselves, School, and World Better)
Week 2	When do you feel bored? What are all the ways you have dealt with being bored? What other ideas might work? (Virtue: Constructive Creativity)	Is it helpful to be positive all the time? Why or why not? (Skill: Social Problem-Solving)	If you were to make a playlist with songs that fit your personality and best describe you, what songs would you choose? Why? (Skill: Communication)	What is one good habit you have? How did you develop this habit? (Theme: Making Ourselves, School, and World Better)	What do you worry about? How can you use Constructive Creativity to worry less? What are some different ways to think about what worries you? (Virtue: Constructive Creativity)
Week 3	What makes you mad? How can you get less angry by using Constructive Creativity? (Virtue: Constructive Creativity)	Discuss how to use "pros and cons" for real-life decision-making using hypothetical situations. Ask students to do the same about a decision they are currently making. (Skill: Social Problem-Solving)	If you were given $1 million, how would you use it to make yourself, school, or world better? (Skill: Social Problem-Solving)	What question(s) do you still have about middle school? What can you do to seek answers to the question(s)? (Skill: Communication)	What is racism to you? What do you think causes racism? How does it affect your life? [This is a tough question, but there are no right/wrong answers!] (Theme: Making Ourselves, School, and World Better)
Week 4	What ideas do you have for an invention? How would your invention improve your life? (Virtue: Constructive Creativity)	If you get into a conflict with a friend, do you usually give in or stand your ground? What other options might you have? (Skill: Social Problem-Solving)	Pick three words that describe you. Discuss the three words with another student in the class and think about your similarities/differences. (Skill: Communication)	If you could only use 10 words to describe what is most important in your life, what would they be? [Consider having all students write their answer to this question and then work in small groups to see if any words on the list were the same] (Skill: Communication)	Who can tell me what violence means? Let's brainstorm as many kinds of violence we can name as possible. [Stress to students that violence is not only physical but can also be done in nonphysical ways. Consider introducing the term "microaggressions."] What can you do to prevent violence around you? (Theme: Making Ourselves, School, and World Better)

December/Month Two (Year 1—*Better Me*): Giving Back to Ourselves, School, and World

	MONDAY	TUESDAY	WEDNESDAY	THURSDAY	FRIDAY
Week 1	Is it easier or harder to understand what someone means when texting? Have you ever had someone misinterpret your words in a text? Do you prefer to text, call, video chat, or speak in person? Why? (Skill: Communication)	Name one thing that someone gave you that matters to you. Why does this item (or action) matter to you? (Virtue: Helpful Generosity)	When you find yourself facing a problem, how do you try to solve it? How do you think things through? How did you learn how to do this? (Skill: Social Problem-Solving)	What is your body language saying right now? How might I know by looking at you if you were actively engaged in the discussion? Once you think about it, is there anything you would want to change? (Skill: Communication)	Think of one thing or object that you really love: maybe your house, your pet, or your phone. What would you do if you were without that thing? How would your life be different? (Theme: Giving Back to Ourselves, School and World)
Week 2	Have you ever written down your feelings in order to communicate them? How was this easier/harder than saying them out loud? (Skill: Communication)	Think of an unexpected act of kindness you have done for someone without expecting anything in return. Was the person thankful? Would you still help others if you were not recognized or thanked for your help? (Virtue: Helpful Generosity)	After solving a problem, how do you know if it was a good choice? What do you do if the choice you made was not a good one? (Skill: Social Problem-Solving)	Oscar Auliq-Ice once said, "If the words you spoke appeared on your skin, would you still be beautiful?" Reflect on that quote. If you knew that this would happen, would you change what you say? How? (Skill: Communication)	What's the most memorable gift you have ever received? What makes it memorable? (Theme: Giving Back to Ourselves, School and World)
Week 3	When listening, we often think of our reply rather than fully hearing a person. How often do you actively listen to someone else? When you don't, why not? (Skill: Communication)	Service could be a simple task like holding a door or offering an open ear for a friend. Think of a time that you were serving others this week. How did they react? Try to notice this more during the rest of this week. (Virtue: Helpful Generosity)	Tell the class about a time that having a plan helped you to achieve a goal. Why was the plan helpful? (Skill: Social Problem-Solving)	What does an enemy mean to you? Do they have power over your day-to-day life? Does using force usually convince someone to not be an enemy? Why or why not? (Skill: Social Problem-Solving)	When was the last time you were proud of yourself? In the past week, what did you do that made someone else proud? Were you proud too? (Theme: Giving Back to Ourselves, School and World)
Week 4	Have you ever made a change that improved your life? What did you do and why did it change you? (Theme: Giving Back to Ourselves, School and World)	If someone followed you around the school for 30 days, what are the three words they would use to describe you? What if they followed you around outside of school? Which words would be more true about you? (Virtue: Helpful Generosity)	Has there been a time someone told you, "Because that's how we've always done it"? Is that a good reason to continue doing something? Why or why not? (Skill: Social Problem-Solving)	What is reliability? If we are not reliable, how will this impact our relationships? How reliable do you think you are? (Virtue: Helpful Generosity)	What is empathy? How do you feel when someone else shows empathy toward you? How do you know when someone is showing you empathy? (Theme: Giving Back to Ourselves, School and World)

January/Month Three (Year 1—*Better Me*): Planning for the Future

	MONDAY	TUESDAY	WEDNESDAY	THURSDAY	FRIDAY
Week 1	A new student just arrived at your school. What do you think it feels like to be living in a new place with all new people? Has this happened to you? (Skill: Empathy)	What is one action you can take in middle school now that will help prepare you for your dream job of the future? (Theme: Planning for the Future)	What is it like to work in a group where others do not communicate effectively to solve a problem? (Skill: Social Problem-Solving)	How can you non verbally demonstrate that you are actively listening to your peers? (Skill: Empathy)	Not every moment in our lives is going to go well, but when bad things happen, we have to try to learn from those situations. Think about a bad moment in your life, and challenge your thinking around how this event helped you. (Virtue: Optimistic Future-Mindedness)
Week 2	Why does it usually feel good to share our feelings with others? (Skill: Empathy)	Pessimism has been related to stress, anxiety, and depression. What could you do today to help combat your negative thoughts and turn them into positive thoughts? (Virtue: Optimistic Future-Mindedness)	If we disagree with someone's perspective, what would be the best thing to do? Have you ever had trouble doing this? (Skill: Social Problem-Solving)	Why might people not listen to new ideas? What helps you be more likely to listen to new or different ideas? (Skill: Empathy)	Is it helpful to think about our past when paving the way for our future? Why or why not? (Theme: Planning for the Future)
Week 3	Who do you admire most? What are some qualities that you admire about this person? (Theme: Planning for the Future)	Small miracles happen every day. What could you do to raise your awareness of these miracles? (Virtue: Optimistic Future-Mindedness)	What does charity mean to you? Do you need to give money, food, or clothing in order to help others? How else can you do it? (Skill: Social Problem-Solving)	What effects can stress have on the body? Why is it important to monitor your stress level? (Virtue: Optimistic Future-Mindedness)	What are you most passionate about? How can you do more of what you love doing? (Theme: Planning for the Future)
Week 4	There are many different ways that help to keep us organized (calendar, planner, etc.). How do you stay organized? (Theme: Planning for the Future)	What is something about your future that you are optimistic about? Why? (Virtue: Optimistic Future-Mindedness)	The person next to you in class keeps trying to look at your paper during a test. What do you do? (Skill: Social Problem-Solving)	What do you like most about being a ____ grader? When do you feel you are at your best in the school? (Virtue: Optimistic Future-Mindedness)	Billy Connolly has said not to judge others unless you are standing in their shoes. Do you agree with that quote? What does it have to do with empathy? (Skill: Empathy)

February/Month Four (Year 1—*Better Me*): Showing Resilience and Overcoming Obstacles

	MONDAY	TUESDAY	WEDNESDAY	THURSDAY	FRIDAY
Week 1	In order to make a change, your voice (thoughts, opinions, and feelings) needs to be heard. Where do you feel like your voice is heard? Are there places where you wish your voice were heard more? How can you make it so? (Virtue: Responsible Diligence)	When experiencing a problem, all people involved have feelings. How do you show your feelings when you are in a conflict with someone? (Skill: Social Problem-Solving)	Self-regulation is the ability to monitor or control your behavior. What do you do to self-regulate in difficult situations? Is there ever a time that it is not possible to self-regulate? (Skill: Emotional Regulation)	What is mindfulness? How could it help you regulate the wide range of emotions you feel in a day? (Skill: Emotional Regulation)	A fixed mindset tells us, "My sadness or disappointment will last forever." A growth mindset would reshape this statement to say, "This will pass as I get back into things." What fixed or permanent thoughts are in your mind about yourself and your life, and how could you reshape them into growth thoughts? (Theme: Showing Resilience and Overcoming Obstacles)
Week 2	Is there one right way to solve a problem? If you believe there are usually multiple solutions, why? (Skill: Social Problem-Solving)	Can obstacles be an opportunity for growth? Why or why not? How might this relate to the recent political climate? (Theme: Showing Resilience and Overcoming Obstacles)	Before making a decision, it is important to think about the positive or negative consequences that might result. Share a time when you did not think of consequences and what you could have done better. (Skill: Social Problem-Solving)	How are you feeling today? Do you take time to reflect on your emotional state throughout your day? How can mindfulness help with this? (Skill: Emotional Regulation)	Effective work requires carefulness and effort, but everyone's minds wander. What do you do to keep your mind focused on the work you are completing? (Virtue: Responsible Diligence)
Week 3	Some have said that the best way to deal with a problem is to solve it yourself. Do you agree, disagree, or are you not sure? Why or why not? (Skill: Social Problem-Solving)	Think of one person you admire. Do they trust in themselves to get through hard times? How do you know? (Theme: Showing Resilience and Overcoming Obstacles)	We all forget things sometimes. What do you do to help yourself take responsibility when you have forgotten to do something related to your schoolwork? To your home responsibilities? (Virtue: Responsible Diligence)	Have you ever reacted with your emotions rather than thinking first? What would you need to do to change your reaction? (Skill: Emotional Regulation)	Before making change, it is important to accept the thoughts, emotions, and situations in your life. What might be one way to help yourself accept a difficult situation? (Theme: Showing Resilience and Overcoming Obstacles)
Week 4	How can someone tell if you are excited? Bored? Can your friends tell? Can your teachers tell? Why does it matter? (Skill: Social Problem-Solving)	What does it mean to have integrity? How does this relate to resilience? (Theme: Showing Resilience and Overcoming Obstacles)	What does it mean to take ownership? Name one situation where you took ownership over a situation. How did you feel about doing this? How have you felt when you did not take ownership? (Virtue: Responsible Diligence)	When can it be important to regulate strong positive feelings, like excitement and happiness? Why? (Skill: Emotional Regulation)	What is your definition of resilience? Who is a friend or relative that you think is resilient? Why? (Theme: Showing Resilience and Overcoming Obstacles)

March/Month Five (Year 1—*Better Me*): Appreciating Ourselves, Our School, and the World

	MONDAY	TUESDAY	WEDNESDAY	THURSDAY	FRIDAY
Week 1	In order to communicate effectively, it is important to listen. While listening, what are some ways that you can ensure that you are understanding? (Skill: Communication)	What is your cultural background? Share one reason you like being part of that culture, or a specific tradition that you appreciate. (Theme: Appreciating Ourselves, Our School, and the World)	Empathy is often defined as including (a) the capacity to share in another's feelings and (b) the ability to understand another's feelings and perspective. Considering empathy in your own life, what is an example when you felt or showed empathy? Why is empathy important in your life? (Skill: Empathy)	One way to practice gratitude is to write a letter or thank-you card to someone you appreciate. Can you share a time when you have done this recently? Name another way that you can practice/have practiced gratitude. (Theme: Appreciating Ourselves, Our School, and the World)	Being grateful often motivates individuals to give back to others. What is one way that you give back to your family, school, or community? (Virtue: Compassionate Gratitude)
Week 2	Do you think there is a difference between a man and a woman's ability to be empathic? Why or why not? (Skill: Empathy)	It is often said that we are our own biggest critics. What is one area of your life where you underestimate your potential? If you shifted your mindset toward appreciation for your talents, how might this impact your life? (Theme: Appreciating Ourselves, Our School, and the World)	What if two people were having a conversation and one person continued to change the subject back to what interests them? How would this impact the other person? How can someone keep from shifting the conversation back to themselves? (Skill: Communication)	What would happen if you did not forgive others in a compassionate way? How might this impact your day-to-day life? (Virtue: Compassionate Forgiveness)	At what age did you start feeling empathy? Share your first memory of being empathic toward another person. Who is someone you feel a lot of empathy for now? (Skill: Empathy)
Week 3	It is often said, "Communication is key." Why do you think this is said? For what is it the key? (Skill: Communication)	We are all unique. How might it hurt you to constantly compare yourself to others? (Theme: Appreciating Ourselves, Our School, and the World)	Think of a time that you showed compassionate gratitude toward someone else. What did you gain from it? How will practicing compassionate gratitude help you in your intended career? (Virtue: Compassionate Gratitude)	Does understanding and using empathy impact your ability to be a successful learner? Why or why not? (Skill: Empathy)	Do you have to try to show compassionate gratitude or does it come naturally? How do you know? (Virtue: Compassionate Gratitude)
Week 4	A person's facial expression can communicate what they are feeling. What are other ways you can communicate nonverbally? Which of these are you most comfortable using? (Skill: Communication)	We often try to show appreciation to others, but do you show appreciation to yourself? How? How can you do this more often? (Theme: Appreciating Ourselves, Our School, and the World)	Do you think it is common for people to be grateful and compassionate in unpleasant life situations? Could it be a helpful way to cope? Why/why not?(Virtue: Compassionate Gratitude)	Some people believe sympathy is when you understand someone else's situation, and empathy is when you feel someone else's feelings in their situation. Do you agree, disagree, or are you not sure? Why? (Skill: Empathy)	What is something about yourself that you think others should appreciate about you? Do you have any friends/family who know this matters to you? (Theme: Appreciating Ourselves, Our School, and the World)

April/Month Six (Year 1—*Better Me*): Connecting With Others and Being a Leader

	MONDAY	TUESDAY	WEDNESDAY	THURSDAY	FRIDAY
Week 1	Earlier in the year we spoke about emotional regulation. A key part of regulating emotions is being aware of when we experience them. For each of these emotions, what are some early warning signals that might let you know these emotions are either present, or starting to intensify? How can knowing these warning signals help you with emotion regulation? (a) Sadness, (b) Anger, (c) Worry, (d) Happiness, (e) Fear, (f) Pride (Skill: Emotional Regulation)	If you are more mindful of your strengths, your self-presentation to others will improve. Think of three strengths you have that would make other people want to be your friend or work with you. As you listen to your classmates' answers, what is one of the three they mention that you think is most clearly true about them, and why? (Theme: Connecting With Others and Being a Leader)	Are sympathy and empathy the same thing? Have you heard people use these terms interchangeably? Do you use the terms that way? Why or why not? (Skill: Empathy)	What are you currently doing in your day to day life to help you better develop yourself as a leader? Ask one of your classmates to tell you more about one of the things they are doing. (Theme: Connecting With Others and Being a Leader)	Do you need an apology in order to fully forgive someone? Why or why not? (Virtue: Compassionate Forgiveness)
Week 2	Empathy is sometimes explained as "standing in someone else's shoes." Think of someone from a different culture, race or religion and discuss how your life might differ. [If someone in the class is of the other culture, race, or religion, it might be helpful to have a reflective discussion] (Skill: Empathy)	What is the role of conflict in being a leader? How comfortable are you with conflict? What are different ways of raising conflicting issues and trying to resolve them? (Theme: Connecting With Others and Being a Leader)	Does emotional regulation happen in your own mind or with the support of an outside perspective? Is it possible to be calm outside of your body but not on the inside? (Skill: Emotional Regulation)	Should the government attempt to provide financial compensation to ethnic and racial groups who were discriminated against historically? If so, would this help those ethnic and racial groups with forgiveness?(Virtue: Compassionate Forgiveness)	Scapegoating means blaming an individual or group for the suffering of others. Can you think of how prejudice may contribute to scapegoating? Can you think of an example from your own life? (Skill: Empathy)
Week 3	Do our emotions influence our actions? Why or why not? If we are in touch with our emotional experiences, can we always control our reactions? (Skill: Emotional Regulation)	Does being connected to someone on social media and in person differ? If so, how? [Consider using a Venn diagram to show similarities and differences.] (Theme: Connecting With Others and Being a Leader)	Is it possible to forgive too much? If so, how do you distinguish the line for "too much"? (Virtue: Compassionate Forgiveness)	"We cannot be true human beings without feeling empathy" (author unknown). What does this quote mean? Consider the family and friends you feel most connected to and how the statement might relate to them (Skill: Empathy)	How do you think refusing forgiveness toward someone can impact your health? [Consider researching stress and health outcomes with your class] (Virtue: Compassionate Forgiveness)
Week 4	Is it always good to regulate your emotions? What are some times when it's most important, and what are some times where it might not be helpful? (Skill: Emotional Regulation)	Where in your life in or out of school do you find yourself connecting with people who are different from you? How do you do this? What challenges have you found in doing this? (Theme: Connecting With Others and Being a Leader)	The only way someone can hurt you is if you allow them to have power over you. Is it possible to avoid this imbalance of power in all situations? If not, give an example when it might be hard to avoid power differences. (Virtue: Compassionate Forgiveness)	Can you think of a time when you wish someone had more empathy for you than they showed? Did you tell them how you were feeling? Why or why not? (Skill: Empathy)	How do you handle criticism? Does it create positive or negative thoughts? How should you handle criticism that is constructive versus criticism that is not helpful? (Skill: Emotional Regulation)

May/Month Seven (Year 1—*Better Me*): Looking Forward: Next Steps on the Journey

	MONDAY	TUESDAY	WEDNESDAY	THURSDAY	FRIDAY
Week 1	When you have difficulty communicating, what helps you to feel more comfortable? (Skill: Communication)	In order to move forward, it is often necessary to consider your choices. Think of a time where you had a choice to make about joining (or leaving) something, or changing your status in some way, and reflect on your decision. What was hard about making the decision? How did it relate to moving forward? (Theme: Looking Forward: Next Steps on the Journey)	Before solving a problem, one of the first things to do is get as many facts about the problem as possible. How might this be helpful to you? (Skill: Social Problem–Solving)	What is one way to plan for an upcoming event? Do you know anyone who does this well? (Theme: Looking Forward: Next Steps on the Journey)	Engaging in service activities often helps people gain a stronger sense of purpose. Have you ever engaged in service? If so, what did you do? How did it help you feel a sense of positive purpose? (Virtue: Positive Purpose)
Week 2	Is every problem solvable on your own? Name a situation where it may be helpful to seek support. (Skill: Social Problem–Solving)	What is something you are looking forward to in the next week? How about in the next year? Why? (Theme: Looking Forward: Next Steps on the Journey)	One way to be an engaged listener is to try to set aside judgment. When you hear things that you do not agree with, how can you avoid criticism and blame? Is this easy to do? (Skill: Communication)	Imagine if you started each day by saying, "Today, I am going to do something that will help me have a positive purpose in my life!" How might your day be impacted? (Virtue: Positive Purpose)	What are the hardest problems to solve between you and your friends? What helps you to solve them successfully? (Skill: Social Problem–Solving)
Week 3	What would happen if you spent more time avoiding your problems rather than solving them? Will the problems eventually go away? Why or why not? (Skill: Social Problem–Solving)	Some say that no matter what, there is always something to look forward to. Do you agree, disagree, or are you not sure? Why? (Theme: Looking Forward: Next Steps on the Journey)	Is it possible for someone to have a negative purpose in life? Why or why not? Are you, personally, able to see a positive purpose for yourself? Regardless, is this a better option? (Virtue: Positive Purpose)	How did the communication between you and your teachers change from second grade to where you are now? What changes would you expect next year? (Skill: Communication)	Bullying is a problem for many students. How might being bullied impact your positive purpose? Do the people bullying have a reason for their behavior? Does that justify their bullying? (Virtue: Positive Purpose)
Week 4	Do you think it is helpful to communicate every thought you have? Why or why not? (Skill: Communication)	"Hope but never expect. Look forward but never wait" (author unknown). What does this quote mean? Do you agree? Why or why not? (Theme: Looking Forward: Next Steps on the Journey)	John Milton once said that "every cloud has a silver lining," meaning that even the worst events or situations have some positive aspect. Do you agree with this? Why or why not? (Virtue: Positive Purpose)	Think of a time when you found it challenging to be working with multiple people to solve a problem. What were the challenges? How did you and the group overcome them if you were able to? (Skill: Social Problem–Solving)	What is your favorite way to communicate with friends? Teachers in school? Your family? (Skill: Communication)

June/Month Eight (Year 1—*Better Me*): Looking Back: What Have I Accomplished? What Have I Learned?

	MONDAY	TUESDAY	WEDNESDAY	THURSDAY	FRIDAY
Week 1	What is something that you are grateful for having done during this school year? [Consider having all students share] (Virtue: All)	What is one thing that MCCs have helped you with this year? (Theme: Looking Back: What have I accomplished? What have I learned?)	How can reflecting on your past help you in your future? (Virtue: All)	Should you look back at only your failures? Only your successes? Both? Why or why not? (Theme: Looking Back: What have I accomplished? What have I learned?)	In the last week, what have you done to help others? Reflect on how this made you feel. (Virtue: All)
Week 2	"Everything you do now is for your future. Think about that" (author unknown). What does this quote mean to you? (Theme: Looking Back: What have I accomplished? What have I learned?)	What is one way that you used your creativity to help you succeed this year? (Virtue: All)	In reflecting on this year, name one way you have taken more responsibility for yourself. How do you feel when thinking back on this success? (Theme: Looking Back: What have I accomplished? What have I learned?)	How would you describe your experience with MCCs in one word? Why did you choose this word? What other word might you use? Why? (Virtue: All)	It is said that we learn something new every day. Do you feel like every experience you have helps you learn or grow? Why or why not? (Theme: Looking Back: What have I accomplished? What have I learned?)

 Available for download at resources.corwin.com/MorningClassroomConversations

Appendix B

Year 2 Daily Prompts

November/Month One (Year 2—*Better School*): Making Ourselves, School, and World Better

	MONDAY	TUESDAY	WEDNESDAY	THURSDAY	FRIDAY
Week 1	Is honesty in school always the best policy? Why or why not? (Skill: Communication)	Imagine some students from another school are coming to visit. What would you tell them and show them about the school so they could understand what it is like to go to school here? (Theme: Making Ourselves, School, and World Better)	Have you ever helped someone in your school or classroom think about a problem in a new way (with Constructive Creativity)? How did you feel after you helped? (Skill: Social Problem-Solving)	What is the biggest problem facing the school right now? How can Constructive Creativity, which involves brainstorming many ways to solve a problem or get something—help? (Virtue: Constructive Creativity)	Finish the sentence: "I care a lot about _____. I think all middle school/high school students should be able to _____." (Theme: Making Ourselves, School, and World Better)
Week 2	What are some positive and negative outcomes to being bored at school? Is there any benefit to boredom? (Virtue: Constructive Creativity)	Do you think staying positive is the best way to deal with setbacks or failure in school? Why or why not? What are ways to solve setbacks or failure when the problems happen in school? (Skill: Social Problem-Solving)	What songs would be on a playlist describing our school? Why? (Skill: Communication)	Have you ever changed a habit related to school for the better or improved something about yourself with regard to school? How did you do that? (Theme: Making Ourselves, School, and World Better)	What do you think is the difference between worrying and being anxious? What are some things in school you worry about? What are you anxious about? How do you handle them similarly/differently with Constructive Creativity? (Virtue: Constructive Creativity)
Week 3	What about the school makes you the most happy? The most upset? How can you do something constructive about what makes you upset about the school? (Virtue: Constructive Creativity)	When trying to solve a problem or make a decision about what to do in the classroom, I usually make a list of pros and cons. What is a decision you are working on with regard to learning in our class? What are your pros and cons? Considering these, what will you decide? (Skill: Social Problem-Solving)	If someone donated $1 million to the school, what would be the first problem you would want to see the money help solve? How do you think it could be used to solve that problem? (Skill: Social Problem-Solving)	What are some questions you have for our school principal? How might you get them answered? (Skill: Communication)	What is poverty? What do you think causes poverty? How does poverty affect our school? [This is a tough question, but there are no right/wrong answers!] [Theme: Making Ourselves, School, and World Better]
Week 4	What is the best school invention of all time? Why? Has it been improved over time? How could you make it even better? (Virtue: Constructive Creativity)	What are the hardest problems that teachers have to deal with every day in school? What do you think are better or worse ways for teachers to solve those problems? (Skill: Social Problem-Solving)	Pick three words that describe this class (or school). Why did you choose these words? [Consider having students work independently or working together as a class to come up with a list] (Skill: Communication)	Do you think any words should be banned from being used in school? Why or why not? (Skill: Communication)	Are there any places in the school or parts of the school day (even coming and going to school) where you worry about being unsafe? What can be done to make those places safer? (Theme: Making Ourselves, School, and World Better)

December/Month Two (Year 2—*Better School*): Giving Back to Ourselves, School, and World

	MONDAY	TUESDAY	WEDNESDAY	THURSDAY	FRIDAY
Week 1	What are some books you own that you could live without? Have you ever thought of donating them to others who don't have as much as you? How would you do it if you wanted to? (Virtue: Helpful Generosity)	Who makes decisions at your school? What would you need to do as a student to have your voice (ideas, feelings, and opinions) heard? (Skill: Social Problem-Solving)	What is the nicest compliment you have ever given someone else? During a given week, how often do you compliment someone at school? (Skill: Communication)	Who is your favorite person in your school and why? Have you ever told this person how they make your life better? (Theme: Giving Back to Ourselves, School and World)	"No one can help everyone, but everyone can help someone." What do you think about this quote? How can it apply to our school? (Virtue: Helpful Generosity)
Week 2	When you give someone a gift, do you expect to get something back? What if we gave freely without expecting anything in return? (Virtue: Helpful Generosity)	What would happen if teachers did not come prepared for class? Why are plans necessary in school? (Skill: Social Problem-Solving)	What was something that you wrote in school or for an assignment that you are especially proud of? What is something that someone else wrote that you have found particularly enjoyable or inspiring? (Skill: Communication)	"Rather than worrying about who was right, be concerned with what was right" (author unknown). Reflect on one thing this week that went well for your school. (Theme: Giving Back to Ourselves, School and World)	Who in this school comes to mind when I say the word "goodness"? What makes this person good? What qualities do you have that others may think remind them of "goodness"? (Virtue: Helpful Generosity)
Week 3	Think of one person in your school who is always there for you. What does this person do that helps you to know they are reliable? (Virtue: Helpful Generosity)	What is one thing that you are grateful for in this school? If you had to live without it for the rest of the year, how would you deal with it? (Skill: Social Problem-Solving)	If you have a phone, imagine your phone broke. What would the school day be like without being able to text/communicate with your friends/family? If you don't have a phone, do you want one? How do you think people used to stay in touch before having mobile phones? (Skill: Communication)	Do you think it is necessary to care for your school? Do students have a role? Are you engaged in any service activities? Why or why not? (Theme: Giving Back to Ourselves, School and World)	Think about a hero or heroine in social studies or history that you have studied in this school. What made this person heroic? Do you consider anyone in the school to be a hero or heroine? (Virtue: Helpful Generosity)
Week 4	"Be the reason someone in your school smiles today." Is making others smile an act of charity? Why or why not? (Theme: Giving Back to Ourselves, School and World)	Have you ever celebrated someone else's success in school? What did you do to show them you were happy for them? (Skill: Social Problem-Solving)	Who in this school has been a good listener to you? How did you know that they were listening to you? (Skill: Communication)	What's the most memorable thing you have done or given to someone in this school? What made it memorable? Does it matter whether the person recognized you did it? (Theme: Giving Back to Ourselves, School and World)	What does the body language of teachers/administrators in this school tell you? Who makes you feel welcomed in the school building? (Skill: Communication)

January: Month Three (Year 2—*Better School*): Planning for the Future

	MONDAY	TUESDAY	WEDNESDAY	THURSDAY	FRIDAY
Week 1	A new student just arrived at your school. What do you think it feels like to be living in a new place with all new people? Has this happened to you? (Skill: Empathy)	Schools often do fundraisers. Think of a fundraiser your school did. Was this fundraiser successful? Why or why not? Brainstorm ways that could improve it. (Skill: Social Problem-Solving)	What do you think it feels like to be a principal? What is the hardest part of their job? (Skill: Empathy)	We learn from our mistakes and we all make them. What is one mistake you made this school year that you learned from? (Theme: Planning for the Future)	The principal is notified that almost a whole class cheated on a recent math test. How should they respond to this problem? (Skill: Social Problem-Solving)
Week 2	Every school has some bad or sad things happen. What can you remember that was bad or sad that happened in this school or a school you were in? How did the school improve as a result, even though it was hard? (Virtue: Optimistic Future-Mindedness)	What was the most productive discussion you have participated in? Did it teach you anything that could apply to this school? (Skill: Social Problem-Solving)	Why is it important to keep an open mind about others' differences? What would happen if we were close-minded at this school? (Skill: Empathy)	Who do you admire most in this school? Have you ever told that person? Why or why not? (Theme: Planning for the Future)	Students are under a lot of pressure. What could you do to make a friend at school smile later today? What about an adult in the school? (Virtue: Optimistic Future-Mindedness)
Week 3	How is coming to this school every day helping you become a more successful and productive adult later in life? (Theme: Planning for the Future)	Where in school do we have the opportunity to share our feelings? How could we create more of these spaces? (Skill: Empathy)	If you disagree with a school rule, what should you do? Could change happen when one person points out a specific problem? (Skill: Social Problem-Solving)	What are some of the values of this school? How can you tell if a teacher/administrator is passionate about that value? (Theme: Planning for the Future)	Every school has potential to be better. What can make this school better from now to the end of the school year? What do you look forward to in your next grade level or school? (Virtue: Optimistic Future-Mindedness)
Week 4	What might happen if the school did not run on an organized schedule? Do you think it would be better or worse? Why? (Theme: Planning for the Future)	Which staff member—other than a teacher—is the best problem solver in the school? Give an example of when you saw this. (Skill: Social Problem-Solving)	In school, it can be difficult to control our impulses or desires to call out. For some, it is easier than for others. What could we do to help decrease the amount of times a day that people talk over each other? (Skill: Empathy)	What is one thing you have learned about how to succeed in this school that you did not know and you wished you knew when you started school? (Theme: Planning for the Future)	If administrators had more open forums to hear how students felt about different issues, would it make the school better? Why or why not? (Skill: Empathy)

February/Month Four (Year 2—*Better School*): Showing Resilience and Overcoming Obstacles

	MONDAY	TUESDAY	WEDNESDAY	THURSDAY	FRIDAY
Week 1	Do you feel your voice is heard in this school? Why or why not? Name one new way to have your perspective considered by others. (Virtue: Responsible Diligence)	Almost everyone has had a time when they went along with a group even though they knew that what they were doing was wrong? Has this happened to you? Why did you go along? What conflicting feelings did you have? What kept you from acting differently? (Skill: Social Problem-Solving)	Is there a certain feeling that you have when entering this school building? Some students feel happy, angry, scared, or excited about their day. Why do you feel that way? What could help make it more positive? (Skill: Emotional Regulation)	Do you believe that all teachers believe in your potential? If so, how do you know? If not, what would you need to change in yourself in order to help teachers see your positive potential? (Theme: Showing Resilience and Overcoming Obstacles)	A French philosopher Jean-Paul Sartre, once said, "Every word has consequences. Every silence too." What does this quote mean? Do you agree that this is true at school? Why or why not? (Skill: Social Problem-Solving)
Week 2	Besides graduating from college, what other types of training do you think teachers receive? How else do teachers prepare for educating students? What would you like to see as part of their training that might not be there now? (Virtue: Responsible Diligence)	If someone asks for help at school, does that mean they are not able to do the work alone? Do you have to be failing to ask for help or attend an extra help session? (Theme: Showing Resilience and Overcoming Obstacles)	Are there certain areas of the school where students are more mindful of their behavior? Do these areas seem more peaceful to you? Why do you say this? (Skill: Emotional Regulation)	Charles Darwin once said, "It is not the strongest of the species that survive, nor the most intelligent, but the one most responsive to change." After COVID-19, when school closed, there has been so much change in schools. Do you agree that adaptability is the most important trait? Why or why not? (Theme: Showing Resilience and Overcoming Obstacles)	Problem-solving occurs every day in schools. Who are the key people you need to communicate with, in order to make progress toward a solution of a problem in school? (Skill: Social Problem-Solving)
Week 3	School starts at the same time every day. Name three ways that you use responsible diligence in order to get to school on time. (Virtue: Responsible Diligence)	Name one difficult experience that you experienced this year at school that you overcame. What did you learn from overcoming this obstacle? (Theme: Showing Resilience and Overcoming Obstacles)	There are times in school when we feel that we are being treated unfairly. When this happens, we need to regulate our emotions and also address what happened. Who in your school would be a person you could go to who could help you with regulating your emotions and help you address the unfairness you experienced? Why did you pick this person? (Skill: Emotional Regulation)	In order to continue to journey forward, it is important to take ownership over your success. That means persisting in areas that are challenging. What is one thing you need to work on before leaving this school? (Virtue: Responsible Diligence)	Students take so many tests in school to monitor their progress. Why is this important? Brainstorm some better ways than relying on tests to show what students have learned. (Skill: Social Problem-Solving)
Week 4	When you notice something going on in school that is not fair, what do you say or do? How much do you persist until someone acknowledges your concern? (Virtue: Responsible Diligence)	What is one rule at school that you have a hard time accepting? What do you do in order to follow that rule? How might you try to get that rule changed? (Theme: Showing Resilience and Overcoming Obstacles)	Teachers have emotions, too. Do you think they respond the same way to emotional situations throughout their lives? Why or why not? (Skill: Emotional Regulation)	Some people say that when something goes wrong in school, it's the adults' responsibility to take care of it. Do you agree or disagree? Why? (Virtue: Responsible Diligence)	The start of the school day is often pretty hectic. Brainstorm some ideas about how to make the start of the school day go more smoothly for everyone. (Skill: Social Problem-Solving)

March/Month Five (Year 2—*Better School*): Appreciating Ourselves, Our School, and the World

	MONDAY	TUESDAY	WEDNESDAY	THURSDAY	FRIDAY
Week 1	It's often easy to complain about things that go wrong in our school. It's a little harder to be thankful for what is going well. What are some things about this school for which you are grateful? (Virtue: Compassionate Gratitude)	At school, how do some of your teachers show you empathy? What makes you feel most understood and comfortable in the classroom? (Skill: Empathy)	If you were asked to explain your school to a student from a different town, what would you say? Which adjectives might you use? How else could you communicate information about your school? (Skill: Communication)	In order to learn effectively, it is important to actively listen. While listening to your teacher, what are some ways that you can ensure that you are understanding? (Skill: Communication)	While in school, do you need to communicate differently with different people (friends, teachers, administrators, etc.)? If so, who and how do you communicate differently? (Skill: Communication)
Week 2	What could we do to show compassionate gratitude to those in our school that are less fortunate than us? (Virtue: Compassionate Gratitude)	Who is the first person in this school that comes to mind when you hear the word, "grateful?" What is one action this person takes which helps them show their appreciation? (Theme: Appreciating Ourselves, Our School, and the World)	As you develop through adolescence, you begin to address conversations in a more mature way. What have you learned that makes you more empathic with your classmates and/or teachers? How has that changed for you since elementary school? (Skill: Empathy)	Each school across this district is unique in its own way. What is one unique quality about your school? How might your school change if this unique quality did not exist? (Theme: Appreciating Ourselves, Our School, and the World)	We often learn through modeling, or watching others do something. Who are the role models for effective communication in school? How do you know that this person is a good communicator? (Skill: Communication)
Week 3	How would the school function if there was no appreciation for materials? (ask for examples of materials—be sure things like books, art supplies, lab equipment, instruments, PE equipment are mentioned)? Would it improve or hinder the student and staff attitudes in the building? (Virtue: Compassionate Gratitude)	Some schools are more diverse than others. What is one positive thing about going to a school with students from many different cultures? (Theme: Appreciating Ourselves, Our School, and the World)	It is often reported that students feel most comfortable in classes that are interactive. When we are having these MCCs, we are allowing ourselves the space to interact. Think of other classes you have. Which ones are easiest for you to communicate in and why? (Skill: Communication)	Think of your favorite performer in music, art, or television. How do you think this individual's school environment impacted their success in their field? What kind of school environment would be most helpful in your future success? (Virtue: Compassionate Gratitude)	Are there any downsides to being empathic at school? Some people believe that it's possible to run out of empathy. What do you think? (Skill: Empathy)
Week 4	Every teacher and staff member has a life outside this school building. Put yourself in their shoes. How do you think they separate their worlds and what would happen if they didn't? (Virtue: Compassionate Gratitude)	Christopher Germer once said, "Self-compassion is simply giving the same kindness to ourselves that we would give to others." Is this something that most people in your school do? How can you tell? (Theme: Appreciating Ourselves, Our School, and the World)	Do you think a teacher/friend of the opposite gender can truly empathize with you? Why or why not, or are you not sure? Do you think gender differences isolate groups of people? Why or why not? (Skill: Empathy)	Think about all of the announcements that come over a school loudspeaker. How would you improve the use of these announcements as a form of communication? (Skill: Communication)	Whose jobs in the school do you think are the hardest? Why? How can you show these individuals your empathy? (Skill: Empathy)

April/Month Six (Year 2—*Better School*): Connecting With Others and Being a Leader

	MONDAY	TUESDAY	WEDNESDAY	THURSDAY	FRIDAY
Week 1	Think of a time in school that you could have used compassionate forgiveness and did not. Reflect on this situation as if you were given a second chance. How might you change your actions? How might this change affect the outcome? (Virtue: Compassionate Forgiveness)	Is empathy needed in order to practice kindness toward others? Why or why not? (Skill: Empathy)	What do you typically do when you feel angry or frustrated? Does this reaction help you and/or others in the long term? (Skill: Emotional Regulation)	Within this school, who would you consider the leaders? Do leaders need to be adult figures in a school building? Why or why not? (Theme: Connecting With Others and Being a Leader)	Do your emotional reactions differ between the home and school environments? Why or why not? (Skill: Emotional Regulation)
Week 2	Should teachers forgive every mistake that a student makes? Why or why not? If not, how could a teacher know the difference between what is forgivable and what is not? (Virtue: Compassionate Forgiveness)	How is your experience as a ____ grader helping you develop yourself as a leader? Are there any barriers to you or your classmates exercising leadership in your school building? (Theme: Connecting With Others and Being a Leader)	Is it easier to practice empathy in certain places in the school or certain parts of the school day? If so, how? (Skill: Empathy)	Connecting with your inner-self impacts your ability to connect with others. Why is this true? How do you connect with your "inner-self"? (Theme: Connecting With Others and Being a Leader)	How do your thoughts about your school impact your experience? If you change your thoughts about what is happening in school, can you change your feelings? (Skill: Emotional Regulation)
Week 3	We practice compassionate forgiveness almost every day, sometimes without even noticing that we are doing it. Do rumors impact your ability to forgive and practice compassion? Why or why not? (Virtue: Compassionate Forgiveness)	How does social media impact a student's connectedness to school? How do you think school was different when students did not have smartphones? (Theme: Connecting With Others and Being a Leader)	Researchers studying happiness are finding that the more you smile at others, the happier they get. Do you agree, disagree, or are you not sure? Why? Assuming it's true, give one example of how you can practice this skill at school. [Discuss how making someone else feel happy can increase your own joy] (Skill: Empathy)	Can compassionate forgiveness apply to your own self? Think of a situation in school for which you did or should have forgiven yourself. (Virtue: Compassionate Forgiveness)	What would help you feel more empathy for things happening to students in school who are different from you? (Skill: Empathy)
Week 4	When you have a disagreement with someone and you forgive them, do you expect their forgiveness in return? What difference does it make to you if they do or do not forgive you? (Virtue: Compassionate Forgiveness)	Are there any reasons why being a leader in your school is not a good choice? Does the setting matter when deciding whether or not to take a leadership role? (Theme: Connecting With Others and Being a Leader)	Who shows you the most empathy in school? Give an example of when this empathy help you through the situation? [This is best done as a pair-share at first.] (Skill: Empathy)	Do teachers and students express their emotional experiences in the same way? Why or why not? (Skill: Emotional Regulation)	Have you seen empathy shown in art, music, or sports? Give an example. (Skill: Empathy)

May/Month Seven (Year 2—*Better School*): Looking Forward: Next Steps on the Journey

	MONDAY	TUESDAY	WEDNESDAY	THURSDAY	FRIDAY
Week 1	Having hope about your potential can impact your ability to succeed in school. Come up with three positive statements you could use in your classroom to help the class believe more strongly in their potential. (Virtue: Positive Purpose)	Think back to your first day of school this year. Have you gained more comfort in communicating your thoughts at school? Why or why not? (Skill: Communication)	Who do you turn to for help when you have a problem to solve related to school? How do they help you? (Skill: Social Problem-Solving)	What do you hope people will say about you once you leave this school? What kind of legacy do you hope to leave behind? Put that into words in one or two sentences. (Theme: Looking Forward: Next Steps on the Journey)	If people avoid problems, what happens? What problems do you feel are currently being avoided at school? Why? What can be done to address them? (Skill: Social Problem-Solving)
Week 2	Positive purpose is often defined as finding an intention to accomplish something useful. What are ways in which you show positive purpose in school? (Virtue: Positive Purpose)	Do students have the opportunity to make choices in school? Does this change from elementary, middle, and high school? If so, how? (Theme: Looking Forward: Next Steps on the Journey)	Sometimes, we can withdraw from situations where we feel uncomfortable and keep thoughts we have in our mind, instead of communicating. Are there any parts of your school day where you find it hard to communicate your feelings? What might be a long-term impact of not communicating? (Skill: Communication)	It is important to continue moving in the direction you would like to go. Does the speed of your movement matter? Why or why not? (Theme: Looking Forward: Next Steps on the Journey)	Acts of everyday courage—tolerance, acceptance, reaching out to those who are different—are not simple. For whom or what are you most willing to fight for, and why? (Skills: Social Problem-Solving)
Week 3	What have you done in this school to serve those around you? In a couple short months, school will be coming to a close for the year. What else can you do before the end of the year to help make the school better? (Virtue: Helpful generosity)	Next year, you will be entering _____ grade (or be a high school graduate). What opportunities do individuals at the next stage of your journey get that you are looking forward to? (Theme: Looking Forward: Next Steps on the Journey)	What are the biggest problems this school will have to solve next year? What are your suggestions for how our school should plan to address these problems? (Skill: Social Problem-Solving)	Think of one positive person in your life. Share with the class one lesson that this person has taught you. Are there ways for you and others to apply this lesson to your time as a student in the school? (Virtue: Positive Purpose)	What are some ways the school can communicate with you so that you are better prepared for the transition to next year? (Skill: Communication)
Week 4	Creating a comfortable environment for students can make school a better place to achieve your goals. Name one way to make your school be a more positive place. How can you help make this happen? (Virtue: Positive Purpose)	C.S. Lewis once said, "There are better things ahead than any we leave behind." Do you think this applies to our school? Why or why not? (Theme: Looking Forward: Next Steps on the Journey)	When there is a problem in school, what are the best ways to gather information to help plan how to solve it? (Skill: Social Problem-Solving)	You are about to transition into a new school year (or out of high school). What feelings are you having about this transition? Have you talked about these feelings before? Why or why not? (Skill: Communication)	What is the most important thing this school can do to help you reach your positive purpose? Are there any ways schools is holding you back now? (Virtue: Positive Purpose)

June/Month Eight (Year 2—*Better School*): Looking Back: What Have I Accomplished? What Have I Learned?

	MONDAY	TUESDAY	WEDNESDAY	THURSDAY	FRIDAY
Week 1	What is something at school for which you are grateful? [Consider having all students share] (Virtue: All)	It is important for a school to reflect on both their successes and failures during a year. What would happen if a school only focused on its successes? Its failures? (Theme: Looking Back: What have I accomplished? What have I learned?)	Many people within this school are helpful. How does being helpful and generous impact the students and staff within a school? Who has been most helpful and generous to you? (Virtue: All)	What is something that you have learned about your school this year that you didn't know before? How will this help you with your transition next year? (Theme: Looking Back: What have I accomplished? What have I learned?)	Who is responsible for making school a comfortable and positive place for staff, teachers, and students? (Virtue: All)
Week 2	What is one thing that you have accomplished to impact this school during your experience with MCCs this year? (Theme: Looking Back: What have I accomplished? What have I learned?)	Name one way that optimistic future-mindedness helps our school. (Virtue: All)	"The expert in anything was once a beginner" (Helen Hayes). What does this quote mean to you? In what areas would you consider yourself an expert? A beginner? (Theme: Looking Back: What have I accomplished? What have I learned?)	Can overcoming adversity make you more creative? Why or why not? (Virtue: All)	What is something this school has taught you about good ways to solve problems? How will this help you in school in the future? (Skill: All)

Available for download at resources.corwin.com/MorningClassroomConversations

Appendix C

Year 3 Daily Prompts

November/Month One (Year 3—*Better World*): Making Ourselves, School, and World Better

	MONDAY	TUESDAY	WEDNESDAY	THURSDAY	FRIDAY
Week 1	Pick a problem in your community right now that matters to you. How could you convince someone to think about this problem in a different way, using Constructive Creativity? (Skill: Social Problem-Solving)	What is the biggest problem facing our country right now? How can Constructive Creativity help? (Virtue: Constructive Creativity)	How do you get informed about the current events of the world? How can you be sure the news you are getting is honest news? (Skill: Communication)	What country do you think has a misunderstanding of how people live in the United States? If you could give a tour to some students from that country, where would you take them and why so they would better understand the United State? (Theme: Making Ourselves, School, and World Better)	What would you be willing to sacrifice (or what would you give up) to make the world a better place? Why? (Theme: Making Ourselves, School, and World Better)
Week 2	Sometimes kids get into trouble when they are bored. Why do you think this is? How can Constructive Creativity solve this problem? (Virtue: Constructive Creativity)	What is the best thing about living in... your town, this state, this country? Why? What are you most optimistic about for the future of this town, this state, this country? (Skill: Social Problem-Solving)	What songs would be on a playlist describing your neighborhood? Why? (Skill: Communication)	What do you think is the biggest health problem facing our country? What good habits would help people face this problem? What can you do about this? (Theme: Making Ourselves, School, and World Better)	What worries you about our country or the world right now? How can Constructive Creativity help with this worry? (Virtue: Constructive Creativity)
Week 3	What upsets you in your community or neighborhood? What can you do that is constructive to make the situation better? (Virtue: Constructive Creativity)	Do you think weighing pros and cons is the best way to make a decision? What other ways have you tried? (Example decisions: pick between two high schools to attend, pick between two sports you'd like to play, or pick either having fun with friends or doing homework) (Skill: Social Problem-Solving)	How important is money to you? How much money does it take for people to be happy? Should we send money to people who have problems, in our town/state/country/around the world? What other ways might help? (Skill: Social Problem-Solving)	What place do you consider the safest place in the world? Why? (Theme: Making Ourselves, School, and World Better)	What questions do you have for the President of the United States? How might you get your questions answered? (Skill: Communication)
Week 4	What is the worst invention of all time? Why? (Virtue: Constructive Creativity)	What are examples of conflicts you are reading about/hearing about in the news? How are people trying to resolve them? How can they do a better job, in your opinion? (Skill: Social Problem-Solving)	Describe the United States to an alien from another planet. Do you think they would want to live here? (Skill: Communication)	What does free speech mean to you? Do you think there should be any limits on free speech? (Skill: Communication)	Many parents don't let kids play with toy guns. Why do you think they do this? Do you think this is a good idea? Why or why not? What about video games involving violence? (Theme: Making Ourselves, School, and World Better)

December/Month Two (Year 3—*Better World*): Giving Back to Ourselves, School, and World

	MONDAY	TUESDAY	WEDNESDAY	THURSDAY	FRIDAY
Week 1	Why do news reports focus so much on negative news? What would you suggest doing differently if anything? (Virtue: Helpful Generosity)	How do groups of people become enemies when they don't even know each other? What do you think can be done to help these groups stop being enemies? (Skill: Social Problem-Solving)	Who in your life is best at talking about problems? Why? (Skill: Communication)	We take things for granted every day. What do you take for granted? Would the world be better if we noticed more things with our senses? Why? (Theme: Giving Back to Ourselves, School, and World)	Do you expect people to be generous to you? Why or why not? Should people expect you to be generous to them? (Virtue: Helpful Generosity)
Week 2	Do you think people are generally charitable? If you were in need in an unfamiliar place, would you trust a stranger to help you? Why or why not? (Virtue: Helpful Generosity)	Who is the most successful person you know? What obstacles did they overcome in order to get to where they are now? (Skill: Social Problem-Solving)	If you could write a letter to one of the most influential people in the world, who would it be and what would you want to say? Why? (Skill: Communication)	Is giving gifts important in your family? Why or why not? Why do you think giving presents is a part of some holidays and not others? (Theme: Giving Back to Ourselves, School, and World)	Men and women volunteer in our country to be a part of the military. What do you think motivates them to do this? (Virtue: Helpful Generosity)
Week 3	Many studies show that people who give to others—whether time or money or help—are happier than those who get things from others. Do you agree or disagree? Why? (Virtue: Helpful Generosity)	There have been many stories in the news about racism and antiracism. Do you feel this is necessary? Is there a story about racism or antiracism that you would like to tell/make sure gets told? (alternative: Think of a news story right now that captured your attention. What reasons do you think the person (or group or country) had for acting the way they did?) [Feel free to expand this prompt to be discussed over several days, if appropriate] (Skill: Social Problem-Solving)	If you look around your community, what type of body language do you see? Do you carry yourself differently inside and outside of school? (Skill: Communication)	Do you think it is necessary to care for the world around you? Are you engaged in any service activities in the community? Why or why not? (Theme: Giving Back to Ourselves, School and World)	Think about a hero or heroine in a news article or story that you have recently read or heard about. What made this person heroic? How might the world differ without heroes and heroines? (Virtue: Helpful Generosity)
Week 4	Imagine that you have been asked to raise money for a local charity. Which charity would you choose, and how would you convince people to donate? (Theme: Giving Back to Ourselves, School and World)	Gratitude is known to improve mental and physical health. Knowing that, what makes it hard for so many of us to practice being grateful? What can help to increase expressions of gratitude? (Skill: Social Problem-Solving)	Do you think cell phones have helped communication for teenagers? What are the benefits? What are the disadvantages? (Skill: Communication)	What is the difference between pride and humility? How would the world be different if it were full of humility or full of pride? (Theme: Giving Back to Ourselves, School and World)	Where in your life outside of school are plans necessary? Who is the best in your family at making plans? Why do you say this? (Skill: Social Problem-Solving)

January/Month Three (Year 3—*Better World*): Planning for the Future

	MONDAY	TUESDAY	WEDNESDAY	THURSDAY	FRIDAY
Week 1	On any news network, we learn so much about the bad events occurring around the world. If you could say one sentence to a news reporter about optimistic future-mindedness, what would you tell them? (Virtue: Optimistic Future-Mindedness)	Think about a time when you have been in a group outside of school and other people are hesitant to speak and discuss. What can you do to make it more likely that they will participate? Why is it important to do this? (Skill: Social Problem-Solving)	There are many people who did not have enough money to afford dinner last night. How do you think they feel? How can other people be helped to recognize this and assist them? (Skill: Empathy)	Who is your favorite historical figure? What have you learned from them? (Theme: Planning for the Future)	What do these words mean to you: idealist; dreamer; pessimist; optimist; realist. Which one or two words do you feel best apply to you? Why? (Virtue: Optimistic Future Mindedness)
Week 2	What is one positive thing that you have done for others this week? How does that help make the whole world a better place? (Virtue: Optimistic Future-Mindedness)	People differ in so many ways like gender, sexuality, religion, race, where they come from, etc. What do we need to do in order to create a safe space for a variety of different people? (Skill: Social Problem-Solving)	Do you have to accept and love all ideas in order to be a loyal member of the United States? Why or why not? (Skill: Empathy)	School is like a job for young people. What skills are you learning in your life as a student that will help you become a better worker one day? (Theme: Planning for the Future)	What are some mental health benefits of feeling comfortable with people from different races, backgrounds, abilities, etc.? (Virtue: Optimistic Future Mindedness)
Week 3	Why do we study history at school? What can we learn from people and events in our past? (Theme: Planning for the Future)	What is corruption? What does it mean when governments are corrupt? What problems does that lead to? What would happen if there was corruption in how schools were run? (Skill: Social Problem-Solving)	Does our social media-filled world create too much emotional sharing? Why or why not? (Skill: Empathy)	Some people believe that each of us creates the future but we are more successful when we create it together. Do you agree? Why or why not? What do you think your role is in creating the future? (Theme: Planning for the Future)	What does it mean to be optimistic? What does it mean to be future-minded? Do they always go together? Why is it good when they do? (Virtue: Optimistic Future-Mindedness)
Week 4	Would you consider the world to be an organized place? Why or why not? What world organizations are you familiar with? What do you think about them? (Theme: Planning for the Future)	We are flooded with images of pain and suffering streaming across the news. What is being publicized that is an example of intolerance, bigotry, bias, or disregard of others? Does not watching help the problem? Why or why not? (Skill: Social Problem-Solving)	If politicians had more open forums to hear the perspective of local individuals, do you think this would make things better or worse? Why? (Skill: Empathy)	"If you don't have a purpose, you don't have a future." What do you think this quote means? How does it apply to your life? (Theme: Planning for the Future)	"Government's job is to problem-solve for the people." Do you agree with this? What involvement have you had with the government in your community to support problem-solving? How do you think the government in your community can do a better job? (Skill: Social Problem-Solving)

February/Month Four (Year 3—*Better World*): Showing Resilience and Overcoming Obstacles

	MONDAY	TUESDAY	WEDNESDAY	THURSDAY	FRIDAY
Week 1	As students, school is your job and it is important that you arrive ready to learn. What would happen if a mayor, governor, army general, or president were having a bad day and arrived at work with a negative attitude? How do you reset a negative attitude? (Virtue: Responsible Diligence)	The fight against hunger has been occurring for years. Do you believe that all problems in the world have solutions? If so, why has the problem of hunger not been solved yet? (Skill: Social Problem-Solving)	Do politicians have the power to change the emotional experiences of people in their communities? States? Countries? Why or why not? (Skill: Emotional Regulation)	The world is full of opportunities, but we must seek them out. Does failure mean you will never succeed? Do successful people ever fail before succeeding? (Theme: Showing Resilience and Overcoming Obstacles)	In the United States, there are plenty of students in leadership positions. How can you become a leader in your community? What obstacles might you face? How can you overcome them? Whose support will help you? (Virtue: Responsible Diligence)
Week 2	Diversity is a very important part of our communities. Although all students are not from the same cultural background, what is one way that your town or neighborhood can demonstrate understanding and appreciating differences in cultures? (Theme: Showing Resilience and Overcoming Obstacles)	What emotions do you feel about problems in your community? Share specific examples. What would change if more people acted on these emotions? (Skill: Social Problem-Solving)	Imagine your favorite place in the world. Using your five senses, describe this place to someone else. Now, think about why you like this place so much. [Consider having students share with a classmate in small groups or partners to allow all to share.] (Skill: Emotional Regulation)	High school is a difficult transition for some students. What is one positive statement you could say to yourself in order to have hope in your potential for the future? (Theme: Showing Resilience and Overcoming Obstacles)	Do you believe all politicians work as hard as they should to make our community and our country a better place? Why or why not? Reflect on what information you used to answer that question. (Virtue: Responsible Diligence)
Week 3	Is it possible to fully forget about a problem that occurred in your past? If yes, how? If not, how does this memory impact the ways communities and countries think about these problems [potentially consider racism, poverty, gender bias, COVID-19, other ongoing issues]? (Theme: Showing Resilience and Overcoming Obstacles)	What motivates citizens to vote? How do you feel about being able to vote in the future? Are there any negative consequences of those who are old enough to vote do not vote? (Skill: Social Problem-Solving)	Some people feel that expressing certain emotions is looked down on in our world. For instance, people might say, "You're weak if you cry" or "Why are you getting excited, that's not a good way to react." Do you think there are some emotions that are looked down on in your family, among your friends, or in your culture? Why? Do you agree? (Skill: Emotional Regulation)	Who is the most authentic person (or the most positive person, the most honest person) that you know? What have you learned from them about resilience? (Theme: Showing Resilience and Overcoming Obstacles)	After a politician makes a decision, is the problem-solving process over? If not, why is it important that they do anything else? (Skill: Social Problem-Solving)
Week 4	John Lewis said that sometimes, it's necessary to get into "good trouble." What did he mean? Do you agree or disagree? Based on this, what are some ways to help those who are having difficulty in your community? (Theme: Showing Resilience and Overcoming Obstacles)	What do you think it feels like to be homeless? What emotions do you think children who are homeless experience? How do you know? (Skill: Social Problem-Solving)	Does self-regulation get easier with age? In other words, is it easier for adults to regulate their emotions than teenagers? Why or why not? (Skill: Emotional Regulation)	If someone tried to keep you from voting, how hard would you try to vote? Why is voting important/not so important to you? (Theme: Showing Resilience and Overcoming Obstacles)	If something in the world was troubling you, how can you let someone know? Brainstorm all the possible individuals, organizations, or groups that you might contact. (Skill: Social Problem-Solving)

March/Month Five (Year 3—*Better World*): Appreciating Ourselves, Our School, and the World

	MONDAY	TUESDAY	WEDNESDAY	THURSDAY	FRIDAY
Week 1	What are warning signs of violence between different groups in your school and/or community? What strategies can be used to prevent violence from breaking out between groups? (Virtue: Compassionate Gratitude)	Are there any conversations at the governmental level that you feel are one-sided? How do you think this could be changed? (Skill: Communication)	What are some ways that our country can improve in the next five years? How will demonstrating empathy impact the success of our country? (Skill: Empathy)	What is one way that you can not only tolerate or accept diversity around the world but instead embrace it? What is the difference between tolerating, accepting, and embracing? (Theme: Appreciating Ourselves, Our School, and the World)	What is one location that you're grateful for in your community? What would happen if this place were closed to the public? (Virtue: Compassionate Gratitude)
Week 2	An anthropologist named Margaret Mead once said, "Never doubt that a small group of thoughtful, committed citizens can change the world; indeed, it's the only thing that ever does." Do you agree, disagree, or are you not sure? Why? (Theme: Appreciating Ourselves, Our School, and the World)	Do local leaders need to show empathy? Why or why not? (Skill: Empathy)	Who are famous individuals you can think of who communicate effectively and how do they do it? Any who don't? What do they do that you most notice? (Skill: Communication)	Norm Kelly once said, "You can't pour from an empty cup." What does this analogy mean? What do you do when your "cup" is near empty and you need to take care of yourself? How can this help us care for others? (Theme: Appreciating Ourselves, Our School, and the World)	Do government officials practice gratitude in public? When? Do you think they should do so more or less? (Virtue: Compassionate Gratitude)
Week 3	What would you consider the best way to communicate with your community if you were a local politician? Why would this work best? (Skill: Communication)	Many scientists now believe that everyone is born with empathy. Do you agree, disagree, or are you not sure? Do you think everyone's empathy—including yours—can be improved? Explain why or why not. If you think yes, how can you improve YOUR empathy? (Skill: Empathy)	There are plenty of people in the world who take for granted the privileges they have. What are some examples of privilege? Knowing the importance of showing compassion and being grateful, what advice would you give privileged people? (Virtue: Compassionate Gratitude)	Not every school gives all of their students equal treatment and equal opportunity. What are some ways you think your school tries to be especially fair to everyone? What happens when schools are not fair? (Theme: Appreciating Ourselves, Our School, and the World)	If you could ask someone from another part of the world to write a blog about their country so you could learn more about it, what country would you pick and what are some things you would want them to blog about? Are there any blogs that you follow now that tell you about what's happening outside this country? (Skill: Communication)
Week 4	Think of groups in your community who are shown less appreciation than others. Reflect on how that impacts your community as a whole. (Theme: Appreciating Ourselves, Our School, and the World)	Do you consider racism to be a problem in your community? In other communities? Knowing this is a difficult topic to communicate about, how would you share your opinion if asked to do so? (Skill: Communication)	Think about the most empathic male and female you know in your community. What is one quality of each that you would like to adopt in your own life? (Skill: Empathy)	Considering the topic of compassionate gratitude, name one way that you plan to "pay it forward" in your life, both in school and beyond. (Virtue: Compassionate Gratitude)	Some people have trouble empathizing with tragic events happening in other parts of the world. Why do you think this is? What would help us feel more empathy for what is happening in other places? (Skill: Empathy)

April/Month Six (Year 3—*Better World*): Connecting With Others and Being a Leader

	MONDAY	TUESDAY	WEDNESDAY	THURSDAY	FRIDAY
Week 1	Think of a time in history where compassionate forgiveness was used. How did this impact the outcomes of the situation, or what happened later? (Virtue: Compassionate Forgiveness)	What does it mean to "regulate?" Across different environments and different cultures, does being emotionally regulated look consistent? How might it differ? (Skill: Emotional Regulation)	In the political world, how is kindness lost? Give one example of unkindness in politics that you are aware of? How could this be improved? (Skill: Empathy)	Leadership is often defined as a twofold concept. It is the ability to analyze your goals/have the self-esteem to carry them out and the ability to guide or direct others. Does this mean that only extroverted, or outgoing, people can be leaders? Why or why not? (Theme: Connecting With Others and Being a Leader)	Name a situation in the world that still requires forgiveness. How might world conflict change if an apology was given? What forms has that taken in history? (Virtue: Compassionate Forgiveness)
Week 2	How has social media impacted the way we view our country and our world? Many of us are able to access news very shortly after it occurs. Is this helpful or hurtful? Why? (Theme: Connecting With Others and Being a Leader)	Sometimes it is hard to put yourself in someone else's shoes. What would you tell a younger student who is struggling with this skill? How might you discuss the skill of empathy with an adult? (Skill: Empathy)	What would happen in our world if all individuals—and especially our leaders—never learned to regulate their emotions? (Skill: Emotional Regulation)	Name three ways that this school could help you better develop as a leader. What would you need in order to effectively enter the workforce feeling like an effective leader? (Theme: Connecting With Others and Being a Leader)	There were wars in our past and there are still wars occurring today. If we all actively practiced compassionate forgiveness, could future wars be prevented? Why or why not? (Virtue: Compassionate Forgiveness)
Week 3	Does media (the news, social media, etc.) impact your feelings throughout the day? Why or why not? Do you think there should be an age requirement for having access to media? Why or why not? (Skill: Emotional Regulation)	Do you think poor people can be happy? Why or why not? Does having more things make you a happier person? Why or why not? Some say it's okay for poor people to have less if they are happy with less. Do you believe this is true? (Skill: Empathy)	Paul Gilbert, a psychologist, once said, "In our definition, forgiveness must be preceded by the ability to empathize with or feel compassion for another." Do you agree or disagree? Why? How might this apply to slavery? (Virtue: Compassionate Forgiveness)	Which political leaders now do you feel connected to? What have they done to help you feel that way? Is there a past political leader you felt connected to? Why? (Theme: Connecting With Others and Being a Leader)	Jonatan Mårtensson once said, "Feelings are like waves, we can't stop them from coming but we can choose which ones to surf." What do you think he meant by this? How do you "surf" your emotional waves? (Skill: Emotional Regulation)
Week 4	How much are you affected by what you hear about the world in the media? Do you feel more connected to good things you hear, or not so good things? Why? (Theme: Connecting With Others and Being a Leader)	In some cases, the actions of others might upset you and you are not given the chance to properly communicate how you feel. In these instances, how else can you handle the situation? (Skill: Emotional Regulation)	How does social media impact our ability to sympathize and empathize? (Skill: Empathy)	After the Holocaust, Elie Weisel said, "I will forgive, but I will not forget." What did he mean? Is forgetting a requirement in order to truly forgive? Why or why not? (Virtue: Compassionate Forgiveness)	When you hear about tragedies happening in other parts of the United States, do you feel empathy? If you were working on a project to assist and serve those involved in the tragedy with other people, do you think your empathy would improve? Why or why not? (Skill: Empathy)

May/Month Seven (Year 3—*Better World*): Looking Forward: Next Steps on the Journey

	MONDAY	TUESDAY	WEDNESDAY	THURSDAY	FRIDAY
Week 1	What kind of service activities do you feel help people most contribute to making the world a better place? Have you ever engaged in this specific type of service? Why or why not? (Virtue: Positive Purpose)	After high school, some of you will go to college, take care of your family members, etc. In thinking about your future, name one way that you plan to improve your communication to make yourself more successful. What do you want people to most know about you? (Skill: Communication)	Are there any problems that you hope to solve before transitioning to high school [college]? What steps would you need to take to help solve that problem? (Virtue: Social Problem-Solving)	Do you have hope for addressing the injustices in this country? Why or why not? (Theme: Looking Forward: Next Steps on the Journey)	Do the local and federal politicians of our world have optimism? Give an example to support your choice. (Virtue: Positive Purpose)
Week 2	Do your goals outside of school and your goals in school need to be the same? If they are different, how might this impact your success? (Theme: Looking Forward: Next Steps on the Journey)	History often repeats itself. How might what you learn in your history classes impact your future? What lessons might your classes teach you about ways to solve problems in the world? (Skill: Social Problem-Solving)	Next year, you will start a new year as a _____ grader [or high school graduate]. How can you use all that you have learned about communication to support this transition? (Skill: Communication)	When you were young, other people made many choices for you. What is one choice that was made that you think has best prepared you to make a positive difference in the world? (Theme: Looking Forward: Next Steps on the Journey)	Regardless of culture, many countries have problems with bullying in school. What is one lesson you have learned in school that you would share with someone trying to tackle the problem of bullying in our world? (Virtue: Positive Purpose)
Week 3	Communicating your thoughts with some people can be easier than communicating with others. Think of a situation, person, or place where you do not feel very comfortable communicating. Why does this place not feel safe sharing your thoughts? Is there a way for you to change this? (Skill: Communication)	Were any international problems in history solved by one person? Give an example to support your answer. (Skill: Social Problem-Solving)	Regardless of your future path, you are going to have obstacles that you will face. How will your positive purpose impact your ability to bounce back from challenges? (Virtue: Positive Purpose)	Every great structure starts with a foundation and builds from there. You had to make a lot of progress to make it to ___ grade. Reflect on your success thus far and name two moments of success for which you are especially proud. If time permits, ask students to reflect also on the foundation on which their success rests. (Theme: Looking Forward: Next Steps on the Journey)	Some problems have been occurring in the world for years. Have we been avoiding them? Why? What do you think of avoidance as a problem-solving strategy? (Skill: Social Problem-Solving)
Week 4	Taking chances can be beneficial, at times. What is something you want to achieve in life that you are willing to take special chances for, in order to be successful? (Theme: Looking Forward: Next Steps on the Journey)	When Martin Luther King, Jr. was young, he did not want to be a preacher. He did not like to communicate to others. How was the world better for his learning to communicate? How will the world be better as you learn to communicate better? (Skill: Communication)	The United Nations was created to help all the countries of the world get together to solve problems. What suggestions would you give to the United Nations to help them be more effective? [Consider visiting the United Nations, online and/or in person as a class if any students are not familiar with it.] (Skill: Social Problem-Solving)	Could your culture and/or where you live impact your ability to believe in your positive purpose? Why or why not? (Virtue: Positive Purpose)	What can students in this school do to address racial tensions within the local community and the world? What will you do? (Skill: Looking Forward: Next Steps on the Journey)

June/Month Eight (Year 3—*Better World*): Looking Back: What Have I Accomplished? What Have I Learned?

	MONDAY	TUESDAY	WEDNESDAY	THURSDAY	FRIDAY
Week 1	Each person has a special talent, skill or understanding that can help the world. Name one talent or skill that is your special contribution to the world. (Virtue: All)	What is one way that you have made a positive impact on the world this year? (Theme: Looking Back: What have I accomplished? What have I learned?)	How would the world change if every person had an optimistic mindset? (Virtue: All)	How does reflection help the problem-solving process? Why is it important for our country and our world to look back at its past realistically? (Theme: Looking Back: What have I accomplished? What have I learned?)	What's one thing this summer that you can do to help make a positive impact on your local community? (Virtue: All)
Week 2	Sometimes it feels like our successes are only powerful on a small scale. What have MCCs taught you about your potential to impact the world around you? (Theme: Looking Back: What have I accomplished? What have I learned?)	In reflecting on this year, name one step you have taken to take responsibility for your school or your community. How do you feel when thinking back on this success? (Virtue: All)	"It's time to discover the deeper mission implanted within you" (author unknown) What does this mean? What steps would you need to take in order to help yourself discover your deeper mission? (Theme: Looking Back: What have I accomplished? What have I learned?)	We have had much discussion this year about gratitude and forgiveness. Is there anyone for which you are newly grateful for or someone you want to forgive? What would make you ready to take this step? (Virtue: All)	What did you learn about the world this past year that you did not realize before? How does knowing this help you for the future? (Theme: Looking Back: What have I accomplished? What have I learned?)

Note: This month intentionally includes two weeks, as assessments/exams and end-of-the-year activities are expected to interfere.

 Available for download at resources.corwin.com/MorningClassroomConversations

Appendix D

Rubrics for Progress Monitoring

MCC Progress Monitoring (Genuine Exchange): Conversation Leader Form

The following chart outlines the components of genuine conversation exchanges so you can monitor progress of students in your group over the course of your MCC implementation. Each skill will be measured on a scale of 1 to 4, relative to your class as a whole. You can highlight or circle your rating for each and tally up totals for each skill or as a whole. Reevaluate at various points throughout your MCC journey to monitor if and how much progress is being seen and for which individuals or subgroups.

Ratings:

1 = Beginning Competence (shows some use of the skill, including when reminded)
2 = Emerging Competence (uses the skill but inconsistently)
3 = Competence (uses the skill regularly)
4 = Exemplar (uses the skill regularly and encourages classmates, serves as a role model)

SOCIAL ETIQUETTE				
Listens without interrupting	1	2	3	4
Actively attends to the speaker with appropriate body posture and eye contact (faces the speaker, directs attention toward the speaker)	1	2	3	4
In small groups/pair-shares, provides appropriate social distance	1	2	3	4

(Continued)

CLARITY				
Expresses thoughts in a clear manner	1	2	3	4
Makes appropriate inquiries of speakers for clarification	1	2	3	4

RECIPROCATION				
In exchanges, respects the integrity of the other person's position	1	2	3	4
Appears open to hearing differing points of view	1	2	3	4
Disagrees without being disagreeable	1	2	3	4

INTEREST AND ENGAGEMENT				
Uses active listening; rephrases others' statements to check for understanding; often takes the form of an "I-message" communications	1	2	3	4
Nonverbally communicates investment by nodding or smiling	1	2	3	4

PERSPECTIVE TAKING AND INCLUSION				
Recognizes others' emotions, especially when one's comments seem to elicit upset in others	1	2	3	4
Treats all others equally—no discrimination based on gender, race/ethnicity, disability status, etc.	1	2	3	4

COMMON GROUND				
Tries to harmonize differences	1	2	3	4
Actively seeks consensus, common ground	1	2	3	4

 Available for download at resources.corwin.com/MorningClassroomConversations

Examining Your Conversation Skills: Student Form

Please read the questions below and circle or highlight your answer on the right. Use the key below and think about what is true for you recently.

1 = Never
2 = Sometimes
3 = Often
4 = Always

CONVERSATION SKILL BUILDING	NEVER	SOMETIMES	OFTEN	ALWAYS
Do you listen to your classmates without interrupting?	1	2	3	4
When a classmate is sharing, do you make eye contact while they speak and turn your chair/body in their direction?	1	2	3	4
When you are part of a small group or with a partner in class, do you give them at least an arm's length of space while working with them?	1	2	3	4
Are you comfortable with expressing your thoughts confidently and clearly?	1	2	3	4
Do you ask your peers thoughtful questions to better understand what they're sharing?	1	2	3	4
Are you open to hearing thoughts and opinions different from your own?	1	2	3	4
When having conversations or disagreements with your classmates, do you express your thoughts in a calm, kind, and respectful way?	1	2	3	4
Do you listen closely to what your classmates share by using your body language or asking them questions about it?	1	2	3	4
Are you able to tell when a classmate is angry, sad, pleased, or frustrated by something you have said or done?	1	2	3	4
Do you treat all of your classmates as equals, despite their background, ability level, or other differences?	1	2	3	4
Do you try to find the middle ground or things in common despite disagreements with others?	1	2	3	4

 Available for download at resources.corwin.com/MorningClassroomConversations

MCC Progress Monitoring (SEL Competencies): Conversation Leaders Form

Please use the following charts on CASEL's five core competencies of SEL to assist you with keeping track of the progress your group shows over the course of your MCC implementation. Each skill will be measured on a scale of 1 to 4, relative to your class as a whole. You can highlight or circle your rating for each and tally up totals for each skill or as a whole. Reevaluate at various points throughout your MCC journey to monitor if and how much progress is being seen and for which individuals or subgroups.

Ratings:

1 = Beginning Competence (shows some use of the skill, including when reminded)
2 = Emerging Competence (uses the skill but inconsistently)
3 = Competence (uses the skill regularly)
4 = Exemplar (uses the skill regularly and encourages classmates, serves as a role model)

SELF-AWARENESS				
Appears to recognize feelings of others, particularly when they are upset	1	2	3	4
Monitors own nonverbal cues to be appropriate to the situation	1	2	3	4

EMOTIONAL REGULATION				
Demonstrates self-control in verbal responses during frustrating situations	1	2	3	4
Maintains a safe body despite anger and temptation of physical outburst	1	2	3	4

SOCIAL AWARENESS				
Shows empathy toward classmates	1	2	3	4
Shows appreciation of others' perspectives or viewpoints, particularly when there are disagreements	1	2	3	4

RESPONSIBLE DECISION-MAKING				
Uses problem-solving to resolve differences with their own interactions or others' interactions	1	2	3	4
Uses problem-solving when faced with interpersonal problems	1	2	3	4

RELATIONSHIP SKILLS				
Shows good informal, rapport building skills at the beginning and end of formal MCCs	1	2	3	4
Contributes to a conversation climate that is respectful, not acrimonious	1	2	3	4

 Available for download at resources.corwin.com/MorningClassroomConversations

MCC Progress Monitoring
(SEL Competencies): Student Form

Please read the questions below and circle or highlight your answer on the right. Use the key below and think about what is true for you recently.

1 = Never
2 = Sometimes
3 = Often
4 = Always

SOCIAL SKILL BUILDING	NEVER	SOMETIMES	OFTEN	ALWAYS
Are you able to tell when a classmate is angry, sad, or frustrated?	1	2	3	4
Are you aware of your body language and how it might appear to others?	1	2	3	4
Do you sense when you are angry or frustrated in time to stop from yelling, saying mean things, or becoming physical with others?	1	2	3	4
Think of the word "empathy" that you have discussed in class. Do you feel that you show empathy to your classmates?	1	2	3	4
Do you show an appreciation of your classmates' opinions, even when you disagree?	1	2	3	4
Do you use problem-solving to resolve differences with your peers, between other people, or in other challenging situations?	1	2	3	4
Do you feel a stronger connection with your classmates during and after MCCs?	1	2	3	4
Do you take part in conversations respectfully?	1	2	3	4
Are you an active group member when working together with your peers?	1	2	3	4
Do you feel comfortable to step up and be a leader in your class?	1	2	3	4

 Available for download at resources.corwin.com/MorningClassroomConversations

MCC Progress Monitoring (Outcomes of MCCs): Conversation Leader Form

This rubric assesses virtues such as Compassionate Forgiveness and Constructive Creativity, which are targeted through MCCs. These ratings can be completed by Conversation Leaders as well as by subject area teachers who are not carrying out MCCs but should be able to indicate the impact of these conversations. This might be completed at the end of each marking period to monitor progress. The questions are worded so that the entire group can be assessed, though the format can be adapted to rate individual students.

Ratings:

4 = True of almost all students in the class/group
3 = True of about half of the students in the class/group
2 = True of a small percentage of students in the class/group
1 = True of almost no one in the class/group

VIRTUE-FOCUSED SKILLS	FEW	SOME	HALF	MOST
Students in my class/group get along well with one another	1	2	3	4
Students work well together in groups	1	2	3	4
Students are more willing to share during academic lessons	1	2	3	4
Students are level-headed with regard to how they speak or act and rarely overreact	1	2	3	4
Students appear to have more confidence when speaking to the class	1	2	3	4
Students engage in productive conversations with their class/groupmates	1	2	3	4
Students engage in productive conversations with me	1	2	3	4
Students are respectful of class/groupmates opinions, even when they disagree	1	2	3	4
Students are receptive to feedback about their ideas and communication style	1	2	3	4
Students appear to be optimistic and have a growth mindset	1	2	3	4

(Continued)

VIRTUE-FOCUSED SKILLS	FEW	SOME	HALF	MOST
Students are willing to be generous to and forgiving of classmates	1	2	3	4
Students are curious and creative and willing to "think out of the box"	1	2	3	4
Students have a clear sense of responsibility as relates to school	1	2	3	4
Students tend to persist in problem-solving, rather than getting thrown off by roadblocks	1	2	3	4
Students appear to have a sense of positive purpose and a good moral compass	1	2	3	4

 Available for download at resources.corwin.com/MorningClassroomConversations

Appendix E

Alternative Implementation Samples (From Chapter 6)

TABLE 6.1 ● December/Month Two in Year 1 (*Better Me*)

	MONDAY	TUESDAY	WEDNESDAY	THURSDAY	FRIDAY
Dec. Week 1	Is it easier or harder to understand what someone means when texting? Have you ever had someone misinterpret your words in a text? Do you prefer to text, call, video chat, or speak in person? Why? (Skill: Communication)	Name one thing that someone gave you that matters to you. Why does this item (or action) matter to you? (Virtue: Helpful Generosity)	When you find yourself facing a problem, how do you try to solve it? How do you think things through? How did you learn how to do this? (Skill: Social Problem-Solving)	What is your body language saying right now? How might I know by looking at you if you were actively engaged in the discussion? Once you think about it, is there anything you would want to change? (Skill: Communication)	Think of one thing or object that you really love: maybe your house, your pet, or your phone. What would you do if you were without that thing? How would your life be different? (Theme: Giving Back to Ourselves, School and World)

This table is a sample week. If you only conduct MCCs three times per week, you might use the prompt for Monday, Tuesday, and Friday. This targets a skill, virtue, and theme.

TABLE 6.2 ● January/Month Three (Year 1—*Better Me*): Planning for the Future

	MCC WEEKLY PROMPT
Week 1	A new student just arrived at your school. What do you think it feels like to be living in a new place with all new people? Has this happened to you? (Skill: Empathy)
Week 2	If we disagree with someone's perspective, what would be the best thing to do? Have you ever had trouble doing this? (Skill: Social Problem-Solving)
Week 3	Small miracles happen every day. What could you do to raise your awareness of these miracles? (Virtue: Optimistic Future-Mindedness)
Week 4	What do you like most about being a ____ grader? When do you feel you are at your best in the school? (Virtue: Optimistic Future-Mindedness)

This table highlights a once-per-week model.

TABLE 6.3 ● January/Month Three (Year 1—*Better Me*): Planning for the Future

	MCC WEEKLY PROMPT 1	MCC WEEKLY PROMPT 2
Week 1	A new student just arrived at your school. What do you think it feels like to be living in a new place with all new people? Has this happened to you? (Skill: Empathy)	"Don't judge others unless you are standing in their shoes." Do you agree with that quote? What does it have to do with Empathy? (Skill: Empathy)
Week 2	If we disagree with someone's perspective, what would be the best thing to do? Have you ever had trouble doing this? (Skill: Social Problem-Solving)	What is it like to work in a group where others do not communicate effectively to solve a problem? (Skill: Social Problem-Solving)
Week 3	Small miracles happen every day. What could you do to raise your awareness of these miracles? (Virtue: Optimistic Future-Mindedness)	Pessimism has been related to stress, anxiety, and depression. What could you do today to help combat your negative thoughts and turn them into positive thoughts? (Virtue: Optimistic Future-Mindedness)
Week 4	What do you like most about being a ____ grader? When do you feel you are at your best in the school? (Virtue: Optimistic Future-Mindedness)	What is something about your future that you are optimistic about? Why? (Virtue: Optimistic Future-Mindedness)

This table highlights a once-per-week model with longer time frames (e.g., 30 minutes), which allows for two prompts.

TABLE 6.4 ● Skill: Social Problem-Solving and Communication

	MCC PROMPT
Session 1	Our group will be taking about 15 minutes at the start of each group to discuss a variety of topics. Some of these topics will be easy to answer and others will make you think deeply. These discussions are going to help us explore our own thoughts and feelings, get to know our group, practice our skills for discussion and respectful debate, as well as several other skills that are crucial for purposeful living. Today, we will start by discussing some rules and expectations for these discussions (the following norms are suggestions that can be adjusted to fit your group, added to your existing norms, etc.): 1. Wait to share your thoughts or answers until it is your turn to speak. 2. Respect others turn to talk by listening quietly and keeping your answers to a reasonable length. 3. Be accepting to others' thoughts and ideas—you may share your disagreements thoughtfully and respectfully, when appropriate and/or if time permits. 4. Use respectful and school-appropriate language. 5. If you have something to share and did not get to, you may share it with me after group, write it down for our MCC box or submit an MCC Google form.
Session 2	Today, we are going to do a self-assessment of our strengths and aspects of our behavior we might want to improve. Take out a piece of paper (or go around the room, dependent on group size) and list at least three personal strengths. How might these strengths impact your success in the group this year? Now, name one area about yourself that you would like to improve. What is something that you will do to be aware of this throughout the group?
Session 3	Describe a time you learned to think about a problem in a new way (with Constructive Creativity). Did anyone help you think in a new way? (Skill: Social Problem-Solving)
Session 4	Can you think of a time you were honest even though it was hard? Have you ever told a harmless lie, just to spare someone else's feelings? Just about everyone has. Does that make you dishonest? (Skill: Communication)
Session 5	Is it helpful to be positive all the time? Why or why not? (Skill: Social Problem-Solving)
Session 6	If you were to make a playlist with songs that fit your personality and best describe you, what songs would you choose? Why? (Skill: Communication)
Session 7	Discuss how to use "pros and cons" for real-life decision-making using hypothetical situations. Ask students to do the same about a decision they are currently making. (Skill: Social Problem-Solving)
Session 8	What question(s) do you still have about middle school? What can you do to seek answers to the question(s)? (Skill: Communication)
Session 9	If you were given $1 million, how would you use it to make yourself, school, or world better? (Skill: Social Problem-Solving)
Session 10	If you could only use 10 words to describe what is most important in your life, what would they be? [Consider having all students write their answer to this question and then work in small groups to see if any words on the list were the same] (Skill: Communication) *Note*: You might want to substitute a revisiting of Session 2 if this were not a focus of this last session, asking students to reflect on areas in which they grew from strength and improved in areas of need.

This table highlights a 10-session model targeting the skills of problem-solving and communication. A model like this might be appropriate for a short-term group or extracurricular activity.

TABLE 6.5 ● Sample of Seven-Week Lunch Group

MCC PROMPT (OPTIMISTIC FUTURE-MINDEDNESS)	MCC PROMPTS (HELPFUL GENEROSITY)
Students are under a lot of pressure. What could you do to make a friend at school smile later today? What about an adult in the school? *(Better School)*	"No one can help everyone, but everyone can help someone." What do you think about this quote? How can it apply to our school? *(Better School)*
Every school has some bad or sad things happen. What can you remember that was bad or sad that happened in this school or a school you were in? How did the school improve as a result, even though it was hard? *(Better School)*	Who in this school comes to mind when I say the word "goodness"? What makes this person good? What qualities do you have that others may think remind them of "goodness"? *(Better School)*
Every school has potential to be better. What can make this school better from now to the end of the school year? What do you look forward to in your next grade level or school? *(Better School)*	Think about a hero or heroine in social studies or history that you have studied in this school. What made this person heroic? Do you consider anyone in the school to be a hero or heroine? *(Better School)*
What is one positive thing that you have done for others this week? How does that help make the whole world a better place? *(Better World)*	Do you expect people to be generous to you? Why or why not? Should people expect you to be generous to them? *(Better World)*
On any news network, we learn so much about the bad events occurring around the world. If you could say one sentence to a news reporter about optimistic future-mindedness, what would you tell them? *(Better World)*	Men and women volunteer in our country to be a part of the military. What do you think motivates them to do this? *(Better World)*
What are some mental health benefits of feeling comfortable with people from different races, backgrounds, abilities, etc.? *(Better World)*	"The happiest people are the givers, not the getters." Do you agree or disagree? Why? *(Better World)*

This table highlights a potential prompt structure for a lunch group.

References

Adams, M., Bell, L. A., Goodman, D. J., & Joshi, K. Y. (2016). *Teaching for diversity and social justice* (3rd ed.). Routledge.

Alber, R. (2015). *20 tips for creating a safe learning environment Classroom management*. Edutopia. https://www.edutopia.org/blog/20-tips-createsafe-learning-environment-rebecca-alber

Ali, D. (2007). *Safe spaces and brave spaces: Historical context and recommendations for student affairs professionals*. http://naspa.org/images/uploads/main/Policy_and_Practice_No_2_Safe_Brave_Spaces.pdf.

Brooks, A. W., & John, L. K. (2018). The surprising power of questions. *Harvard Business Review, 96*(3), 60–67.

Chiaramello, S., Mesnil, M., Muñoz Sastre, M. T., & Mullet, E. (2008). Dispositional forgiveness among adolescents. *European Journal of Developmental Psychology, 5*(3), 326–337.

Collaborative for Academic, Social, and Emotional Learning. (2013). *2013 CASEL guide: Effective social and emotional learning programs: Preschool and elementary school edition.*

Collaborative for Academic, Social, and Emotional Learning. (2015). *2015 CASEL guide: Effective social and emotional learning programs: Middle and high school edition.*

Collaborative for Academic, Social, and Emotional Learning (CASEL). (2018). *What is SEL?* https://casel.org/what-is-sel/

Damon, W., Menon, J., & Cotton Bronk, K. (2003). The development of purpose during adolescence. *Applied Developmental Science, 7*(3), 119–128.

Domitrovich, C. E., Durlak, J. A., Staley, K. C., & Weissberg, R. P. (2017). Social-emotional competence: An essential factor for promoting positive adjustment and reducing risk in school children. *Child Development, 88*(2), 408–416.

Durlak, J. A., Domitrovich, C. E., Weissberg, R. P., & Gullotta, T. P. (Eds.). (2015). *Handbook of social and emotional learning (SEL): Research and practice.* Guilford.

Dutro, E., & Bien, A. C. (2014). Listening to the speaking wound: A trauma studies perspective on student positioning in schools. *American Educational Research Journal, 51*(1), 7–35.

Elias, M. J. (2010). School climate that promotes student voice. *Principal Leadership, 11*(1), 22–27.

Elias, M. J. (2013). *A call to all social-emotional learning leaders*. Edutopia. https://www.edutopia.org/blog/call-to-all-sel-leaders-maurice-elias.

Elias, M. J., & Arnold, H. A. (Eds.). (2006). *The educator's guide to emotional intelligence and academic achievement: Social-Emotional Learning in the classroom.* Corwin.

Elias, M. J., Leverett, L., Duffell, J., Humphrey, N., Stepney, C. T., & Ferrito, J. J. (2015). Integrating social-emotional learning with related prevention and youth-development approaches. In J. A. Durlak, C. E. Domitrovich, R. P. Weissberg, & T. P. Gullotta (Eds.), *Handbook of social and emotional learning (SEL): Research and practice* (pp. 33–49). Guilford.

Elias, M. J., & Nayman, S. (2019). Students taking action together: Using social emotional competences to build civility and civic discourse. *NJEA-Feature Review.* https://www.njea.org/student-taking-action-together-stat/

Elias, M. J., & Tobias, S. E. (2018). *Boost Emotional Intelligence in students: 30 flexible, research-based activities to build EQ skills.* Free Spirit.

Fielding, M., & McGregor, J. (2005). *Deconstructing student voice: New spaces for dialogue on new opportunities for surveillance? Paper presented at the Annual Meeting of the American Educational Research Association.* Quebec.

Fullan, M. (2005). *Leadership and sustainability: Systems thinkers in action.* Corwin.

Gale, B., Mazor, J., & Harrell, A. (2017, Fall). Developing/running transdiagnostic social skills intervention programs for children and adolescents. *The Los Angeles Psychologist*, 8–9.

Hatchimonji, D. R., Linsky, A. V., & Elias, M. J. (2017). Cultivating noble purpose in urban middle schools: A missing piece in school transformation. *Education*, 138(2), 162–178.

Hatchimonji, D. R., Linsky, D. R. V., & Elias, D. R. (2019). Frontiers in youth purpose research. *Journal of Character Education*, 15(2), vii–xviii.

Kozol, J. (1991). *Savage inequalities: Children in America's schools.* Harper Perennial.

Krahenbuhl, K. (2020). In class discussions, slow and steady wins. *Educational Leadership*, 77(7), 28–33.

Kriete, R., & Davis, C. (2014). *The morning meeting book.* Center for Responsive Schools, Inc.

Levin, B. (1994). Educational reform and the treatment of students in schools. *Journal of Educational Thought*, 28(1), 88–101.

Malin, H. (2018). *Teaching for purpose: Preparing students for lives of meaning.* Harvard University Press.

McArthur, B. A., Burke, T. A., Connolly, S. L., Olino, T. M., Lumley, M. N., Abramson, L. Y., & Alloy, L. B. (2019). A longitudinal investigation of cognitive self-schemas across adolescent development. *Journal of Youth and Adolescence*, 48(3), 635–647.

McClain, K. (2019). *Exploring SEL mediation: Student-teacher relationships may be a necessary component for academic success in urban middle schools* (Publication No. 13881526). [Doctoral Dissertation, Fairleigh Dickinson University]. PQDP Open. https://www.proquest.com/docview/2236091528

Morton, J. (2020). *What is a brave space? North Carolina State University Office for Institutional Equity and Diversity.* https://diversity.ncsu.edu/news/2020/04/02/what-is-a-brave-space/

Munley, P. H. (1975). Erik Erikson's theory of psychosocial development and vocational behavior. *Journal of Counseling Psychology*, 22(4), 314–319.

Murphy, N. A., Yuan, M., & Elias, M. J. (2020). Youth leadership programming in high-poverty minority students. *Evaluation and Program Planning*, 79, 1–10.

Novick, B., Kress, J. S., & Elias, M. J. (2002). *Building learning communities with character: How to integrate academic, social, and emotional learning.* ASCD.

Pawlo, E., Lorenzo, A., Eichert, B., & Elias, M. J. (2019). All SEL should be trauma-informed. *Phi Delta Kappan*, 101(3), 37–41.

Perkins, D. (2003). *King Arthur's roundtable.* Wiley.

Rudduck, J., Chaplain, R., & Wallace, G. (1996). *School improvement: What can pupils tell us? David Fulton.*

Rutgers SECD Lab. (2018). *What is SECD?* https://www.secdlab.org/

Ryan, R. M., & Deci, E. L. (2000). Self-determination theory and the facilitation of intrinsic motivation, social development, and well-being. *American Psychologist*, 55(1), 68–78.

Schieble, M., Vetter, A., & Martin, K. M. (2020). *Classroom talk for social change: Critical conversations in English language arts.* Teachers College Press.

Simmons, D., & Simmons, D. (2019). Why we can't afford whitewashed social-emotional learn-ing. *ASCD Education Update*, 61(4). http://www.ascd.org/publications/newsletters/education_update/apr19/vol61/num04/Why_We_Can't_Afford_Whitewashed_Social-Emotional_Learning.aspx.

Skipper, Y., & Douglas, K. (2015). The influence of teacher feedback on children's perceptions of student-teacher relationships. *British Journal of Educational Psychology*, 85(3), 276–288.

Taylor, R. D., Oberle, E., Durlak, J. A., & Weissberg, R. P. (2017). Promoting positive youth development through school-based social and emotional learning interventions: A meta-analysis of follow-up effects. *Child Development*, 88(4), 1156–1171.

Templeton, J. M. (2002). *Wisdom from world religions.* Templeton Press.

Vieno, A., Santinello, M., Galbiati, E., & Mirandola, M. (2004). School climate and well-beingin early adolescence: A comprehensive model. *European Journal of School Psychology*, 2(1–2), 219–238.

Wangaard, D., Elias, M. J., & Fink, K. (2014). Educating the head, heart, and hand for the 21st century. *SEEN: Southeast Education Network, 16*(2), 16–19.

Weis, L., & Fine, M. (Eds.). (1993). *Beyond silenced voices: Class, race, and gender in United States schools.* State University of New York.

Weissberg, R. P. (2019). Promoting the social and emotional learning of millions of school children. *Perspectives on Psychological Science, 14*(1), 65–69.

Index

A SAGE Publishing Company

Helping educators make the greatest impact

CORWIN HAS ONE MISSION: to enhance education through intentional professional learning.

We build long-term relationships with our authors, educators, clients, and associations who partner with us to develop and continuously improve the best evidence-based practices that establish and support lifelong learning.

Solutions YOU WANT | Experts YOU TRUST | Results YOU NEED

EVENTS >>> **INSTITUTES**

Corwin Institutes provide large regional events where educators collaborate with peers and learn from industry experts. Prepare to be recharged and motivated!

corwin.com/institutes

ON-SITE PD >>> **ON-SITE PROFESSIONAL LEARNING**

Corwin on-site PD is delivered through high-energy keynotes, practical workshops, and custom coaching services designed to support knowledge development and implementation.

corwin.com/pd

>>> **PROFESSIONAL DEVELOPMENT RESOURCE CENTER**

The PD Resource Center provides school and district PD facilitators with the tools and resources needed to deliver effective PD.

corwin.com/pdrc

ONLINE >>> **ADVANCE**

Designed for K–12 teachers, Advance offers a range of online learning options that can qualify for graduate-level credit and apply toward license renewal.

corwin.com/advance

Contact a PD Advisor at (800) 831-6640 or visit www.corwin.com for more information